UNCHARTED

UNCHARTED

A Rediscovered History of Voyages to the Americas Before Columbus

Tim Wallace-Murphy

James Martin

NEW
PAGE

This edition first published in 2023 by New Page Books, an imprint of
Red Wheel/Weiser, LLC
With offices at:
65 Parker Street, Suite 7
Newburyport, MA 01950
www.redwheelweiser.com

ISBN: 978-1-63748-011-3
Library of Congress Cataloging-in-Publication Data

Names: Wallace-Murphy, Tim, author. | Martin, James
(Paranormal investigator), author.
Title: Uncharted: a rediscovered history of voyages to the Americas before Columbus /
Tim Wallace-Murphy and James Martin. Description: Newburyport, MA:
New Page, 2023. | Includes bibliographical references. | Summary: "The Americas
have had native groups living there for more than 10,000 years, but Columbus was
surely not their first visitors. This book covers a range of cultures who had seemingly been visiting the Americas since long before Columbus. Evidence is explored of
potential Roman and Phoenician shipwrecks off the coast of South America through
to Celtic and Norse exploration of Northern America. With source materials dating
back through millennia, including very recent finds, this book will induce the reader to
think about a side of history still readily dismissed by some"— Provided by publisher.
Identifiers: LCCN 2022051074 | ISBN 9781637480113 (paperback) |
ISBN 9781633412965 (kindle edition)
Subjects: LCSH: America—Discovery and exploration—Pre-Columbian. |
BISAC: BODY, MIND & SPIRIT / Ancient Mysteries & Controversial Knowledge |
HISTORY / North America
Classification: LCC E103 .W36 2023 | DDC 970.01/1—dc23/eng/20221209
LC record available at https://lccn.loc.gov/2022051074

Cover design by Howard Grossman
Interior by Steve Amarillo / Urban Design LLC
Typeset in Crimson Pro and Europa

Printed in the United States of America
IBI
10 9 8 7 6 5 4 3 2 1

For Tim Wallace-Murphy:
The world lost a friend; we lost a father.

Contents

Preface   ix

Dedications   xiii

Introduction   xv

1   Fantasy versus Fact   1

2   Corn in Egypt and Egyptians in the Americas   11

3   Classical Greece and the Roman Empire   27

4   The Celts   35

5   The Viking Voyages: Myth or Reality?   43

6   Transpacific Contact   59

7   Maritime Trade in Europe I: The Mediterranean   69

8   Maritime Trade in Europe II: The Western Coasts   79

9   Baron of Roslin and Earl of Orkney   87

10 The Earl Consolidates His Power   95

11 The Zeno Exploration of the North Atlantic   105

12 A People of Peace   113

13 The Voyage to Vinland   121

14 The Most Controversial Building in North America   131

15 Dissension, Discussion, and Debate   145

16 Celebrating History   157

17 Controversy over the Zeno Narrative   167

18 Columbus: Discoverer of the New World?   173

Notes   177

Index   197

Preface

The origins of this book started around 2014, with Tim wanting to write a follow-up to the "great book, but strangely named *Templars in America*," as he put it. This book would chronicle, as best as possible, humanity's exploration of the Atlantic and Pacific oceans, in discovering the Americas before the time of Columbus. The focus was to source as best as possible and describe the exploration by various peoples to the Americas prior to 1492.

Over a period of months, Tim began to coalesce his thoughts on the outline of the book. Soon he had produced the manuscript for this book, which, with some editing and additions, would have been ready for print. He decided not to do anything with the manuscript. It remains a mystery to me as to why he chose to do nothing with the book. I had asked why he hadn't wanted to progress the book, but more important projects awaited, he explained. Because I cared for Tim over the last few years of his life (alongside others), and because he was very much a fatherlike figure to me, some have suggested that he wanted to give this manuscript to me to complete—just as Trevor Ravenscroft had once done for him, something to which Tim had alluded to me on a few occasions.

My real involvement in this book began in 2016–20 while sitting at our favorite coffee shop in Quillan, France. Tim had begun to discuss a stalled project that he had been working on relating to proposed pre-Columbian transatlantic voyages. I remember that we had started our customary coffee that day at around 9:30—espresso for Tim, a café crème and a *jus d'Orange* for me. We were joined by a mutual friend, a vicar from the southwest of England, and as was often the case, by the time we had finished our morning coffee, it was afternoon. Imagine the scene: two historians and a vicar locked into deep discussion. I can only imagine how our conversation must have sounded to a fly on the wall. By the close of the day, I had agreed to undertake an edit of the manuscript, and over the coming months, emails bounced between the two of us with different edits. It wasn't too long before I sought his permission to add a few sentences, then a few paragraphs, and then finally a few chapters.

As I complete this work at the start of 2022, during the turbulence of the COVID-19 pandemic, I find myself reviewing the email exchanges between us, with one especially Wallace-Murphyesque line having made me chuckle: "well, you can add what you like to the book, dear boy, I can always delete it afterwards"—Tim even to the last. With this said, and more puzzling, whenever I attempted to discuss the additions and edits with him, as I wanted to do ever so frequently, I was met by the phrase "be in a slow hurry, dear boy" or "let's look at it later." With this in mind, "a slow hurry" would be the best title for this book! I suppose I should begin some sort of introduction.

The topic of pre-Columbian transatlantic exploration, other than a mouthful to say, is, to many, an exciting if not controversial one. Serious academics very seriously hold to the view that prior to Columbus, the notion of European or Asian travelers having any form of contact with the Americas is ridiculous. This said, however, developments and finds from the Americas that would be commonplace in Europe or Asia simply cannot be ignored or automatically dismissed as ridiculous. We present to you evidence—and, yes, in some places speculation—that Columbus really didn't discover anything unknown. The Western-centric model of exploration deserves to be examined and other cultures respected. Furthermore, our modern view that ancient peoples were somehow backward, unsophisticated, or incapable is a notion simply untrue. We have used evidence in this book from a wide range of temporal periods and, given the sensitivities of the term *exploration*, which for some led to genocide and occupation, have attempted to be respectful and aware of the hardships faced by so many. With this in mind, in completing this book, I have sought to remember those who have—and still to this day do—suffered under conditions in which history still has taught us no lessons.

Our mission in this book is not necessarily to educate, but it is to provoke, and to provoke you into thought about a side of history still so readily dismissed by some. I have attempted to capture both my own and Tim's passion for this topic, and as such, I have, where possible and with evidence, looked to further the notion that "They Did Not Come to Conquer."

Tim—you asked me to edit, then add to this book, and—it seems in conversations you had with others—left for me to complete. I hope I have done you proud.

James Martin

Dedications

From Tim Wallace-Murphy
For Niven Sinclair

From James Martin
For Max—you are my world and my rock; thank you for supporting
me as ever with this project. I would also be remiss if I did not
mention Tigson, Tim, Thor, and Douglas; you have each kept
me company and, on occasion, listened to my thoughts.

For my family—thank you for your support and for being there, through
thick and thin. Mum, Mike, Billy, and Elizabeth, thank you for everything.

For René, Jeannie, David, Gill, Trevor, and Patrick—thank
you for proofing, reading nonstop additions, listening to
my explanations, and also being a great support.

For Sean, Colin, Michael, Jack, and others—I know that, when
teaching, I deviated from Law, Industrial Relations, OSH, etc.,
and often into history—it helped. And we had fun.

For Rick, Barry, Lynne, and Malcolm—sounding off ideas and frequently
delving into history with you has massively helped in completing this work.
And thank you to the many others who have supported us both throughout.

Introduction

There is a principle which is a barrier against all
information, which is proof against all arguments and
which cannot fail to keep a man in everlasting ignorance—
that principle is contempt prior to investigation.

—Herbert Spencer

Contempt prior to investigation and outright denial of reality are not attitudes restricted to fundamentalists of the religious or political persuasion alone. Sadly, this form of distorted thinking also infects parts of the academic world. This realm, which traditionally extols the virtues of proof, hard evidence, logical argument, and open-mindedness, is far from immune from a degree of denial that almost beggars belief. Nowhere is this more evident than in the study of early voyages to America. The "official" academic view that "Columbus was the first European to reach the New World" seems to be written in tablets of stone. It is not merely the dominant theory; it is the only one that is seriously discussed by American and European historians. The massive array of hard evidence to the contrary that has emerged over the past century or more has been denied, derided, ignored, or condemned as fake. When an artifact such as the Vinland Map, for example, is discovered, it is loudly and publicly denounced as a forgery. This announcement makes headline news and reinforces the public perception that "Columbus was first." Whereas the later proof of its authenticity is reported only in obscure journals that ordinary citizens never read, and thus, this news rarely impinges on the public consciousness.

A significant corollary to the concept that "Columbus was first" is the definitive and equally rigid idea that there was no dissemination of native American flora and fauna to the outside world until after 1492. The academic bias in favor of Columbus is also invariably applied to any artifact found within the United States, irrespective of its age or nature. If it is dated prior to 1492, it will be described as "of Native American origin," ignored, or misfiled. For example, in 1943 James Howe bought a farm on the banks of the Roanoke River in Virginia. He found some bog iron on the farm and some slag and guessed that he had stumbled across the traces of an old colonial forge. However, he could not find any records to substantiate this use, which was rather odd as such a forge would undoubtedly have been important enough to be recorded. He continued his search and found over 400 pounds of iron and a natural draft furnace. He then began to excavate more carefully and found various quantities of iron at a depth of 80 centimeters. At that level he also discovered a superb bronze cup in relatively good condition, two more fragments of bronze, and a bronze spindle. Finding bronze artifacts among the iron debris led to the conclusion that they must have been imported. Iron ore can be found in the locality, but neither tin nor copper, the constituent elements of bronze, occurs anywhere in the vicinity.[1]

Comparative studies of the bronze cup began to reveal some interesting facts. Six cups of a similar type and of comparable metallurgy were found in the ruins of Pompeii and have been dated to a few years before the Common Era, indicating that they are over 2,000 years old. A nearly identical cup, also found in the U.S., is on exhibit in the Smithsonian Institution, and it is labeled with no date—merely a question mark! It is simply one such misleadingly labeled artifact among so many others on display there. An iron nailhead found at a Roman site near Saalfeld Fort in Germany is dated as being manufactured about 200 BCE. An identical nailhead found in America and exhibited in the Smithsonian again carries no date but merely another question mark.[2] Yet, paradoxically enough, it was a professor from that very Smithsonian Institution who finally broke ranks and made a breach in the wall of denial erected by American academics on the subject of pre-Columbian voyages to America. He did it using archaeology and modern science, namely DNA studies.

The theory first put forward by Dennis Stanford, chairman of the Anthropology Department of the Smithsonian Institution and Bruce Bradley, an independent researcher, in 1999 is referred to as the "Solutrean hypothesis." Stanford and Bradley claim that some of America's early inhabitants crossed the Atlantic from Europe a little more than 18,000 years ago from an area that encompasses Spain, Portugal, and southwestern France. They were part of a tribe known as the Solutreans, who, it is proposed, settled in the area now known as the present-day U.S. Eastern Seaboard. The Solutrean hypothesis claims that over the next 6,000 years, their hunting and gathering culture spread to the American deserts and the Canadian tundra and perhaps into South America. Evidence for this spread is found in the distinctive style of their projectile points and other clues within the archaeological record. Comparing projectile points from both Europe and Asia, Stanford and Bradley hypothesize that the Solutreans were the first settlers who brought to North America what was previously known as "the Clovis culture."

DNA records support the Solutrean hypothesis, as mitochondrial DNA testing revealed some unexpected links between Europe and North America. Three percent of Native Americans who were tested have mtDNA from a different haplogroup than the others whose mtDNA is from haplogroups A, B, C, or D.[3] This haplogroup of the 3 percent, called X, was found to be particularly high in some tribes, such as the Ojibwas of the Great Lakes. Genetic anthropologists state that the presence of X in North America points to an early migration from Europe. Furthermore, by examining the mutations within haplogroup X, scientists are able to use that "genetic clock" to estimate when these early Europeans arrived, and they have come up with two time ranges—either between 36,000 and 23,000 years ago or between 17,000 and 12,000 years ago.

Despite the staunch and steadfast denial by the American historical establishment of even the possibility of any transatlantic voyages prior to 1492 CE, two respected scientists have now broken ranks and had the temerity to suggest a high degree of probability for an early voyage from Europe to America when mankind was primitive, to say the least, and boatbuilding skills were in their infancy. Other DNA studies indicate that the ancestors of the Native American peoples who crossed the land bridge across the Bering Strait from Asia pushed an existing population southward as they spread throughout the continent. The descendants of these displaced peoples now inhabit Tierra del Fuego, and their DNA indicates a Polynesian origin. Thus, modern science has blown a hole a mile wide in the official position that Columbus was first by proving that both the Atlantic and Pacific oceans had been crossed during that mysterious time known as prehistory. Let us now examine in some detail the vast body of hard evidence for transoceanic voyages that has been so summarily dismissed or ignored by American academics since Columbus was officially declared the first to discover America.

CHAPTER 1

Fantasy versus Fact

We live in a fantasy world, a world of illusion.
The great task in life is to find reality.

—IRIS MURDOCH

Oscar Wilde once famously declared, "Many people discovered America before Columbus, dear boy, but most of them had the good sense to keep quiet about it." Most early visitors to the New World indeed did keep quiet about it; they came for trade and profit and thus needed to protect their source of supply in order to maintain a business monopoly. Transatlantic and transpacific voyages were frequent and are recorded in the mythology of Central and South American religions, in pre-Columbian art, and in hard archaeological fact. Yet, American academic opinion denies this absolutely and makes the rigid and dogmatic allegation that Columbus was the first to cross the Atlantic in 1492 and that diffusion of native American flora and fauna has occurred only since then. For any American academic to question this rigid belief is to commit professional suicide as a historian in the U.S. This has resulted in another flawed archaeological axiom: "The ground rules for archaeology state specifically (albeit they are unwritten) that any site that pre-dates 1492 in the U.S. must be Native American in origin and cannot possibly have been occupied by anyone else prior to that date."[1] It has been argued elsewhere that the primacy of the Columbus voyage is "proven" by the lack of any bona fide evidence to the contrary. That is not to say that there is no such evidence, but rather that all contrary evidence has been condemned, dismissed, or devalued by the academic hierarchy, who are supposedly the custodians of public education.[2]

In this work we shall summarize some of the more compelling evidence that has been discovered by scholars and researchers of repute who absolutely refute this blinkered attitude. We will also detail the shipbuilding and navigational skills employed by these ancient mariners, cite the economic imperatives that provoked their voyages, and list the evidence to be found on both sides of the ocean that proves, irrefutably, that Columbus was a latecomer to transatlantic exploration.

An essential part of the Solutrean hypothesis was the rationale that drove these people to move. During the last years of the Ice Age, hunter-gatherer societies were even more vulnerable than usual to variations in the food supply. So, when that was nearing exhaustion, they had one simple and brutal alternative: "Move or Starve."[3] According to Stanford and Bradley, the Solutreans sailed in skin boats, skirting the edge of the polar ice cap and living off the sea life, just as much as the modern-day Inuit people still do. Eventually, they reached the shores of North America and began to spread, ultimately mixing with the local population.

The economic imperative provides a vital key in understanding why groups of people move, travel, and seek to trade with one another. Future historians could not plausibly begin to understand the complexities of our modern-day international relations without first accepting and understanding our current dependence on oil to fuel our economies. Nor, for example, can we, looking back to the Victorian era, attempt to understand the harshness of Victorian life without understanding their society's reliance on iron and coal, which was the mainstay of their economy. It has ever been thus. The reliable supply of whatever was considered as the vital ingredient for life, prestige, or prosperity is the key to understanding the survival of our species and the rise and fall of empires throughout history. This was even more important in the distant past when technology was in its infancy and when mankind had not yet learned enough about metallurgy to smelt metallic ores. In the early Bronze Age before man had discovered the art of smelting copper and tin, sources of raw natural copper and alluvial tin were vital. These were the raw materials for all metal tools, agricultural implements, and, above all, weaponry. The twentieth-century arms race between the old super-powers of Russia and the U.S. was nothing new; in fact, it was a situation as old as the history of civilization itself. In his masterwork, *Studies in Ancient Technology*, R. J. Forbes remarked, "Much of ancient history could be rewritten as a struggle for the domination of quarries and ore deposits or metal supplies."[4]

Developments in the history of metallurgy always dictate what kind of mineral deposit is exploitable and at what date. In the Bronze Age, the skill of the smiths permitted them to use only stream or alluvial tin and not vein cassiterite. The relatively few sources of alluvial tin juxtaposed to copper in the enormous quantities that were required—not just for armies, but for adornment, for agriculture, and for tools—made the steady and reliable supply of these metals absolutely vital.[5] In fact, writing in *A History of Technology*, Singer suggests that it was not until Roman times that vein cassiterite could be used, therefore survival in the Bronze Age absolutely depended on finding supplies of alluvial tin.[6]

Reliable and plentiful supplies of copper are equally essential, and natural copper deposits from around the world take the following form: on the top of the deposit is pure or native copper; below that, oxidized copper such as malachite; below that, an enriched sulfide zone containing impurities like arsenic; and below that, sulfides alone. Therefore, finding a cheap source of copper was the lure that launched the quests of mariners from the ancient Middle East who sailed all over the world's oceans. These exploratory voyages began in the sixth millennium BCE and didn't stop until the Iron Age. The secretive nature of these explorations and the trackless nature of the world's oceans kept this knowledge from the history books.

Once the traders had learned of the location of the New World resources, they ensured that the commerce across the oceans continued for their own personal profit. The world's largest deposits of native copper were found, and can still be found, near the Great Lakes of North America.[7] There are only two places in the world where native copper occurs naturally in abundant quantities, and both are in the Americas. The smaller is in Bolivia, near the headwaters of the Amazon; the other, which produces vast quantities, is at Lake Superior at the Upper Peninsula of Michigan and on the lake island of Isle Royale. Mining and the fashioning of copper weapons were carried on there from the sixth millennium BCE to 1000 BCE. This dating is very significant indeed, because it indicates that the use of copper began at about the same time in America as around the Black Sea and the Middle East. If this use is simply a coincidence, it is a very strange one—especially as the stone mauls used for shaping and forming the copper were of a type used for early metalworking in the Old World.[8] The mines on Isle Royale did not go out of use until 1000 BCE. Just as we cannot account for the supply of native copper used in the Old World without allowing for the exploitation of this North American source, also we can find no evidence in the New World that anything like enough metal was used there to account for the actual output of the mines. The North American metal was exported, although, as the years went by, more copper came to be used in the Americas.[9] It has been estimated that the workings at Isle Royale and the Upper Peninsula of Michigan represented a total production of between 250,000 and 750,000 tons of copper. Apparently, no one knows who the miners were, but a Chippewa oral legend claims that their forefathers drove out a white race, which might have been the miners.[10]

At the beginning of the Bronze Age, arsenical bronze was the first development, but it was soon found to be too dangerous to handle and, as a result, tin bronze began to come into use from 3500–3200 BCE. Egypt started using bronze sometime about 2600 BCE. However, the sources of ancient Egyptian and Cypriot tin are supposedly unknown.[11] We should state that there were only two possible sources for the amount of alluvial tin needed: West Africa, from present-day Ghana, is one possibility, and the other, and most probably the principal source, is vast amounts of accessible alluvial tin from the Amazon Basin in South America.

Ocean Crossing

One common misconception that tends to inhibit understanding of the maritime skills of our early ancestors lies deeply rooted in the land man's fear of the sea. Those with no maritime experience simply do not know that it takes far less energy to transport goods over water than it does over land. Furthermore, the same people do not know the power or the reliability of ocean winds and currents. These two facts have distorted our perceptions for far too long. Because of the trackless nature of the sea, comparative distances are also difficult or impossible to estimate by the landlubber. For example, most people labor under the false assumption that it is easier to traverse the Mediterranean from end to end than to cross the Atlantic—yet the distance from shore to shore across the Atlantic is actually shorter than the length of the Mediterranean. Crossing the Atlantic is actually easier than traversing the Mediterranean. The pattern of winds and currents makes crossing the Atlantic and the subsequent return voyage to Europe relatively easy. The two great almost-circular currents ensure this, aided and abetted by the prevailing winds. Anyone sailing off the coast of Africa who just left their craft at the mercy of the elements would almost inevitably be taken by the currents and the prevailing winds to the Caribbean. The circular patterns of the currents and winds would then again take the craft across the Atlantic in the direction of the British Isles via the Gulf Stream.

Whether or not the first people to sail across the Atlantic did so by design or by accident will never be established, but cross it they did, in great numbers and repeatedly over a prolonged span of time. This can be stated with complete confidence, as the evidence for these voyages can be found in abundant quantities on both sides of the ocean. For example, some American archaeologists have estimated that over half a million tons of copper were removed from the mines near Lake Superior, yet only a tiny proportion of this has been located in burial mounds and archaeological sites actually on the American continent. American author and researcher Gunnar Thompson speculates that the bulk of the copper was exported overseas.[12] Another bizarre anomaly has yet to be explained. Assays made and reported in 1991 show that some of the copper artifacts found in North

American burial mounds were not made from pure copper at all, but from zinc-copper alloys of Mediterranean origin.[13] Who were these ancient ocean travelers and who were the principal intercontinental traders? Did they leave any discernible traces or evidence of their visits to the Americas?

The Phoenicians dominated early transatlantic trade, but by the beginning of the second millennium BCE, the Minoans of Crete and Thera (now Santorini) were also heavily involved in trade that reached across the north Atlantic Ocean to Mexico and further north to the Great Lakes. They were the principal carriers of pure native copper that originated from upper Michigan and Isle Royale. The role of the Minoans in bringing metals and corn (maize) across the Atlantic is confirmed by two gold corncob rings that were found at an archaeological site in Crete and dated to the second millennium BCE.[14] Writers from ancient Egypt described the "two-way" river of the ocean that had the capacity to carry vessels rapidly across the sea and from America.[15] We will later describe a considerable body of evidence that demonstrates that Egypt initiated its own transatlantic voyages and was not entirely dependent on Phoenician or Cypriot traders. Furthermore, Harold Sterling Gladwin repeatedly drew attention to cultural features and objects, particularly pottery, that demonstrate that several American tribes had contact with parts of the Old World, such as the Mediterranean as well as the Orient. The various artistic styles that he listed point to direct voyages between the Old World and America over 2,000 years ago.[16]

In our investigations, we need to research the travels of both the Minoans and Phoenicians. They traded with and supplied the ancient empires of Egypt and Babylon. In fact, for almost the entire Bronze Age, the Egyptians were largely dependent on Phoenician merchant ships that brought ingots of copper and tin from the New World.[17] The Phoenicians, who were as poor in metals as the Egyptians, made fortunes out of the maritime metals trade.[18] Indeed, a model of the Phoenician god Melqart was found in Rio Balsas, Mexico.[19] Furthermore, there was an identification of Hittite glyphs on obsidian discs by Mrs. Ruth Verrill in the state of Utah.[20] Archaeologists and explorers have found Phoenician inscriptions in Peru as well as ceramic portraits of the ancient mariners. Semitic people in ancient Peru?[21] The ancient visitors from Phoenicia carved graffiti on stone mauls, boulders, and memorial tablets that were found in the Amazon Basin and all across the eastern United States. These Punic-Iberian travelers were more literary than their Minoan predecessors; after all, they gave us our alphabet. These Amazon carvings are within the vicinity of the principal tin deposits that were exploited in the Bronze Age. The doctrinaire scholars, who have been unable to locate the ancient sources of tin that were used in the Old World to make bronze, may need to cast their nets further afield and look across the Atlantic Ocean.[22]

The relationship between the black leaders of Egypt and the Phoenicians around 670 BCE may help to explain how a Mediterranean figure with a flowing beard and turned-up shoes appears in association with black figures in ancient Mexico and how certain elements of Phoenician artifacts—including the model of the aforementioned Phoenician god Melqart—have been unearthed in the Americas, within contexts that are related to the African-Egyptian presence there.[23]

The largest oceangoing ships, at the height of Phoenician power, were built at Tartessus on the Atlantic coast of Spain. This port was where tin was imported and stored, before being further shipped onward to its final destination. Homer wrote that tin came out of the Atlantic and, as we have already mentioned, at that time there were only two sources that could supply the alluvial tin in the vast quantities necessary—one being in Africa and the other in the Americas.[24] Epigraphers use the word *Tartessian* to describe the script that its residents used, a paleo-Hispanic language that proves to be no more than a dialectical version of Phoenician. The ships of *Tarshish*, a term that eventually came to signify a type of ship and one capable of long sea voyages, were the largest seagoing vessels known to the Semitic world—long sea voyages indeed, as Tartessian inscriptions have been found in New England (such as those at Mount Hope Bay, Bristol, Rhode Island), West Virginia, and Ohio.[25] The first authenticated find of an engraved Phoenician tablet in a North American archaeological context was a Tartessian inscription found in 1838 and excavated from a burial chamber at the base of Mammoth Mound in Moundsville, West Virginia. Although the Tartessian alphabet had not then been deciphered, the similarity of the inscription to Iberian writing was recognized, and in the contemporary reports of the dig, the mound and its contents were attributed to European visitors.[26] Further east, on the island of Corvo in the Azores, a pot full of Phoenician coins dating from 330–320 BCE was discovered in 1749.[27]

Bimini Road

The Bimini Road, also known as the Bimini Wall, is a strange underwater rock formation off the coast of North Bimini island in the Bahamas. The structure consists of a 0.50-mile-long northeast-southwest linear feature composed of roughly rectangular limestone blocks, resembling a road or harbor wall. Although the "road" is generally considered to be a naturally occurring geological feature, there is still some debate surrounding the possibility that it is in fact a man-made structure—possibly that of an ancient road or wall. This theory is one championed by Robert Marx and Dimitri Rebikoff, who believed that the structure at Bimini was a sunken wall or perhaps even the remnants of an Atlantean city.[28] We must point out at this stage that normally we would run a million miles when hearing any mention of Atlantis. This said, however, a variety of intriguing finds and similarities to other ancient sites may link our Phoenician ancestors to the Bimini Road.

In 1969, marine engineer and oceanographer Dimitri Rebikoff asserted that the Bimini Road formation was similar, if not identical, to numerous other ancient man-made harbors discovered throughout the Mediterranean.[29] Finds such as stone anchors and harbor foundations found at Cosa, Italy; Akko, Israel; and Samos, Greece (among others) appear similar to the apparent stone anchors and harbor-like structure at Bimini. Cosa, Akko, and Samos were also sites visited and occupied by the ancient Phoenicians, Romans, and Greeks. If these ancient groups had indeed traveled to the New World, they may have used similar harbor construction techniques that were commonplace in the Mediterranean at Bimini. Away from the hypothesis that the structure is a harbor, author Frank Joseph asserts that the structure in fact resembles the massive ancient walls found at the Phoenician and Roman site of Lixus in today's Morocco.[30]

The ancient site of Lixus

While there are some similarities between numerous ancient sites and the Bimini complex, it is difficult to come to a solid conclusion on the nature of the site. Could it be man-made? Or is it evidence of the beauty of nature? The only conclusion that can be brought to this discussion is that further investigation of the structure is required. If future evidence emerges that concludes the site is man-made, then we shouldn't look to an Atlantean hypothesis. The site has been carbon-dated to being between 2,000 and 4,000 years old. We could perhaps consider the notion that this is a Phoenician port situated off the coast of the United States. The age of the structure would fit within the Phoenician and Roman period, and it may have sunk beneath the waves. Whatever the nature of Bimini, we should keep an open mind to possibilities; however, for the time being, evidence points toward a natural phenomenon. Time will tell.

CHAPTER 2

Corn in Egypt and Egyptians in the Americas

Jacob saw that there was corn in Egypt....

GENESIS 42:1

S ome children who have grown up in the Western world since the advent of universal education are familiar with the expression "corn in Egypt." It is one of the most familiar biblical quotes of them all. The question that arises from that expression is one of supreme importance to isolationist and diffusionist academics alike—"What plant does the word *corn* refer to?" To diffusionists, it is held to mean maize, or Indian corn, a plant native to the Americas. To the isolationists, it is a generic term that refers to wheat and any other European or Middle Eastern native grain. This potentially vexatious question was apparently answered in the early years of Egyptology when a Swiss botanist, Alphonse de Candolle, conducted a somewhat cursory study of carvings of ancient Egyptian temples in 1885. Having toured a few tombs in Giza, he asserted definitively that there was absolutely no reliable evidence of maize agriculture in Egypt, or anywhere else in the Old World, until after Columbus's first voyage in 1492. Significantly, it was only after this fateful pronouncement had been made that the isolationist scholars proclaimed that it was Columbus alone who was responsible for the transmission of American flora and fauna to worldwide diaspora. Apparently, no one in the isolationist camp ever questioned how, on the basis of such a cursory and incomplete survey, de Candolle could state so definitively that there was no evidence of maize agriculture either in Egypt or elsewhere in the Old World. His word was taken as final and absolute. Before we examine the wealth of evidence that proves de Candolle to be just plain wrong, let us have a brief look at the fate of those scientists and academics who have the integrity and courage to question the prevailing party line that "Columbus was first."

Scholars who report evidence that is contrary to the New World Isolationist Paradigm are immediately ostracized. When Smithsonian archaeologist Betty Meggers found Japanese ceramics at an Ecuadorian site, she dated the pottery to the third millennium BCE. Thus, Japanese ships had sailed across the Pacific and established a colony in South America. Despite that fact that her evidence, methodology, and conclusions were beyond reproach, her colleagues promptly denounced Dr. Meggers. Of course, being a woman in a so-called male occupation did not aid her cause. When Eben Norton Horsford found evidence of a Nordic colony in New England, the novelist Samuel Eliot Morison roundly castigated him. When African-American scholar Professor Ivan Van Sertima reported evidence of voyages to ancient Mexico involving black Africans, he was ridiculed as a "racist" in an anthropological journal. Thor Heyerdahl is still regarded by some Norwegian scholars as a "pseudoscientist and crackpot" for suggesting that Egyptians could have sailed to Mexico. The fundamentalist attack squads ridiculed former British submarine commander Gavin Menzies, who claimed that Ming Chinese admiral Zheng He had sailed around the world almost a century before Columbus. Menzies was promptly condemned by many anthropologists and historians, despite the vast amount of evidence supporting his thesis.[1]

Japanese pottery?
(Source: Museo LP 503 Estilo Valdivia, *commons.m.wikimedia.org*)

All reasonable hypotheses in any academic context should always be subjected to rigorous peer review by other scholars, but that review should be not merely deep and analytical but also fair, reasonable, and open-minded. Let us now muddy the waters of the diffusionist/isolationist arguments with a few uncomfortable facts. Firstly, let us establish how plant species can cross nearly 3,000 miles of ocean. Let us take maize for our primary example. Seeds or kernels from the domesticated maize plant are too large to be transported by migratory birds. Furthermore, the corncobs could not float by themselves all the way to Europe, Africa, or Asia—and if they did, they would be ruined by prolonged immersion in salt water. If the biblical expression "corn in Egypt" does refer to maize, then it would constitute solid proof that ancient mariners from the Middle East had crossed the Atlantic Ocean and returned, many centuries before Columbus.[2]

The question is "When did maize, a New World plant, first reach the Old World?" If Old World traders succeeded in sailing between their home ports and ancient America, then they may have significantly influenced the rise of New World civilizations and provided an essential food supply to the empires of the Old World. From the evidence that has been garnered from ancient Egyptian temple carvings, New World maize reached the Middle East at the apparent dawn of civilization.[3] We do not have to rely on the carvings of maize to prove that it was a common crop in ancient Egypt; actual corncobs have been found, very early on when Egyptology was in its infancy. As early as 1819, Egyptian archaeologist J. J. Rifaud reported that maize had been found inside a sarcophagus, a previously unopened casket that was nearly 3,000 years old.[4] The earliest carvings of corncobs occur in tombs that were constructed during the reign of Pharaoh Snefru (a.k.a. Sneferu, 2620–2547 BCE).[5]

Columbus's first voyage in 1492 undoubtedly opened up the Americas to European conquest and bestowed upon Spain a vast hoard of New World gold. What Columbus did not do was bring the world's most important food plant, maize, to the Old World—that had actually happened about 5,000 years earlier. It was maize, or Indian corn, that fed the Jews during the famine in the second millennium BCE; that enabled the Persians to build an empire in the Middle East during the fourth century BCE. Maize originated in the Americas, but the crops that fed the Jews, the Romans, and the Persians were grown in Egypt. European traders had sailed across the Atlantic Ocean, taken the New World crop back to the Middle East, and used it to feed its people. No other grain had the level of productivity to produce the enormous shipments of surplus grain to overseas customers.[6]

Many diffusionist scholars have listed compelling evidence that maize had reached India, Africa, and China long before the first voyage of Columbus.[7] Indeed, Indian corn was one of the major ingredients of human cultural evolution in the Near East, because it provided such a vast and dependable food supply wherever it was planted. No other crop is as versatile in terms of adapting to new habitats: it sustained the growth of populations and fed legions of soldiers, laborers, and slaves upon whose backs civilization was brought forth from the bounty of Mother Earth in the Middle East.

American historian Gunnar Thompson and his colleagues have established conclusively that the ancient Egyptians farmed maize extensively at a very early date. The evidence they have discovered demonstrates that maize farming was firmly established along the Nile River by about 5000 BCE, a revelation that will come as a profound shock to traditional-minded academics all across the world. Thompson and his team have identified over 400 corncobs in carvings in the ancient tombs or drawn on the papyrus scrolls of Egypt. Several hundred more have been identified on artifacts from a variety of archaeological sites situated elsewhere in the Middle East, such as in Babylon and Uruk in ancient Iraq. The earliest maize agriculture coincides with the introduction of metal-edged plows and is depicted as "cornrow farming." This form of agricultural technology using "corn drills," "corncribs," and "corn threshing" is distinctly different from the traditional methods of cultivating small grain crops such as wheat, barley, and so on. Farming wheat, barley, or oats involves field hoeing and broadcast seed scattering—not sowing individual grains in holes placed in a drill. Also, small grain farmers stored their harvest in bags or granaries, not in "cribs."[8]

When in the National Museum in Edinburgh, Thompson saw a red and black vase from the Naqada I era among a collection assembled by Cyril Aldred.[9] A stylized corn plant could clearly be seen on the surface. The image consisted of large droopy leaves that were arranged along the side of a stalk that was topped by the distinctive crown of tassels that is commonly seen on maize plants. Aldred had traveled extensively in Egypt and had amassed an extensive collection of photographs and artifacts that he later donated to the museum. Among the photographs from the temple of Queen Hatshepsut, Thompson found an image of a Nubian servant carrying a tray of fruits and vegetables, surmounted by the spectacular shape of a corncob with husk leaves. An examination of more recent color photographs from this same temple has confirmed that the cobs are painted yellow, while the husk leaves are green. The cob itself is covered with raised circles that mimic the surface texture of kernels on actual corncobs. The temple carvings are dated to approximately 1470 BCE. Revisiting the British Museum, Thompson was astonished by what he found—dozens of depictions of maize plants that he had signally failed to notice on previous visits.[10] These examples included a New Kingdom glass vase (circa 1250 BCE) with a corn plant motif and several limestone memorial tablets with stylized maize ears. In the British Library he also found a papyrus scroll called *The Book of the Dead*, decorated with fowl, fruits, and vegetables in mortuary displays for the afterlife. The scroll dates to the New Kingdom era circa 1250 BCE. One mural from the queen's temple had been copied in a painting by the distinguished Egyptologist Howard Carter in 1909 that clearly showed three distinct maize cobs. Thus, there can be no doubt whatsoever that maize was extremely well established in ancient Egypt. Thompson and his colleagues found many examples of earlier pottery from the Naqada I phase (c. 4000–3500 BCE) decorated with schematic paintings of maize plants. These can be found in a variety of collections in the British Museum, the Ashmolean Museum, the Metropolitan Museum of Art in New York, and in the Museum of Egyptian Antiquities in Cairo.

These questions arise from this vast array of evidence:

> Were the ancient Egyptians merely the beneficiaries of trading nations such as the Phoenicians or the Minoans?
>
> Did they ever cross the Atlantic themselves?
>
> Or, indeed, did they have suitable ships or the ability to build them?

Carvings in the temple of Hatshepsut at Djeser-Djeseru portray five enormous oceangoing vessels all constructed from Lebanese cedar. These are well over 100 feet long, broad in the beam, equipped with a triangular mast and four steering oars at the stern. The mast supported a single huge flaxen sail that, when fully extended, reached out from both sides of the vessel for at least 10 feet. The use of the sail in this position was suitable only for downwind progress; however, the sail could also be rigged in a lateen configuration that enabled the vessel to sail crosswind. It is a matter of record that, around 2600 BCE, Pharaoh Snefru sent an expedition overseas to an unknown destination described as "the land of Punt." Sahure's expedition to Punt followed in 2460, Mentuhotep III's expedition sailed in 2000 BCE, and Hatshepsut's expedition to the same destination took place in about 1470 BCE. Thompson and other historians have speculated that these voyages to Punt were, in fact, to Central America.[11] We know, from the work of Bailey and others, that an ancient script used by Libyans and Cretans has been found in the Amazon River Basin.[12] Let us now examine the Egyptian records of these voyages to the land of Punt and then progress to an investigation as to what evidence can be found in the Americas of ancient Egyptian visitors.

The standard explanation by historians for the location of the land of Punt is that it is at some unidentified point on the east coast of Africa. Yet Egyptian records indicate that those who went there followed the setting sun. If it were simply left to the indications we find in Egypt, this matter would still be in dispute. The carvings supposedly depicting the land of Punt that can be found in the temple of Queen Hatshepsut at Djeser-Djeseru are inconclusive, to say the least. However, the accounts of the cargoes brought back from Punt shed a little light on the problem. Pharaoh Sahure is reported to have received 80,000 baskets of antyu incense that may well have been copal incense from Mexico. For real proof, however, we have to traverse the Atlantic and study one of the most mysterious civilizations in Central America, the Olmecs.

Insofar as we can establish, the Olmec civilization of Mexico first emerged on the east coast shore of the Gulf of Mexico near the San Lorenzo pyramid. From about 1500 BCE, this became the capital of an empire that ultimately spread all across Mexico from coast to coast, reaching southward to present-day El Salvador. Apparently, ancient Egyptian exploration of this region may have begun in the reign of Pharaoh Snefru around 2600 BCE. However, the Egyptians were not the only voyagers interested in the vast wealth of this region for, by 1000 BCE, Shang Chinese were in the western provinces. One intricately carved stone pillar from Alvarado shows a black African captive and an Asian chieftain. It is one of many clues to the

Corn in Egypt and Egyptians in the Americas

battles that were fought over the control of trade. A variety of traders from many countries brought silks, spices, slaves, iron, and tools that they bartered for native drugs, jade, turquoise, copper, lapis lazuli, and gold. There are numerous clues that African seafarers reached the shores of Mexico in that era. They include

> The oldest iron tools found in America
>
> *Tumbaga*, a copper-gold alloy (sometimes referred to as the green gold of Emu)
>
> Numerous portraits of Africans carved in stone
>
> The so-called Olmec heads

The colossal Olmec stone heads of Africans have been found at La Venta, Tres Zapotes, and San Lorenzo. A very distinctive design of a bronze axe was made in Egypt that was pierced so as to leave a figure, molded in relief, framed by the edge of the blade. The Olmecs used an absolutely identical design.[13] The question of where the native people of Central America, the Olmecs or the Maya, got their hard-edged iron tools to do such intricate stone carving has been studiously avoided by the isolationist school. As has another related question: How can even the most ingenious artist paint or sculpt people of another race he has never seen? But a plethora of stone statues are scattered among the Olmec sites in Mexico, showing distinctly non-native features. Indeed, the first Europeans to see them knew that they were looking at people from outside America. One type is portrayed with African features, whereas another type, found farther north, is depicted in a different way, often with a goatee. A Mayan vase from Guatemala shows both types together. One old temple displayed the stone carving of a man's head with strikingly European features, which probably represents one of the white gods.[14] The hard-edged metal tools that Mexican artisans needed for making these incredibly intricate carvings must have come from Egyptian or Phoenician merchants.

Dr. Matthew Stirling did the principal excavations of the so-called Olmec head. In 1938 he led a joint team of Smithsonian and *National*

Geographic scholars to a point just outside the village of Tres Zapotes near the Gulf of Mexico. He found enough evidence to secure the funding for another expedition in 1939, which unearthed some of the most remarkable finds in American archaeological history. The first head to be found was huge, carved from a single block of basalt. The workmanship was described as "delicate and sure," and the head is an accurate portrait of a Nubian face surmounted by a ritual helmet. Nearby a stele was found that was dated to 291 BCE. Later, larger heads of a much earlier date were to be found. In another expedition a year later, Stirling excavated the more important site of La Venta. Four more huge Nubian heads were discovered there. These sites were not carbon-dated until 1955 and 1956. The results were startling—814 BCE plus or minus 134 years, an era that spans the time of the twenty-fifth dynasty in ancient Egypt. Chisel marks, confirming the use of iron tools, were discovered on the base of one of these carvings by Gunnar Thompson. Also found at the same site was a carving of a Mediterranean-type figure standing beside them, carved out of a stele, with a flowing beard and turned-up shoes.[15] Evidence of a purely African contact with pre-Columbian America was established in 1970 by Professor Alexander von Wuthenau, professor of art at the University of the Americas in Mexico City.[16] He has described his discovery of a considerable number of heads fashioned in clay, copper, copal, and gold with Nubian features. These were found in a variety of strata whose dates ranged from the earliest Central American civilizations up to 1492 and are of unquestionable African influence. The facial features and tattoo markings are unmistakable and skillfully recorded.[17] American writer and historian Frances Gibson, while dated in language, wrote that African "colonies were found in Panama when the Spaniards arrived. The white man, the black man and the red man in the costume of the Indian of North America, and the yellow man are all depicted on the murals of Chichen Itza."[18]

At the great temple site of Monte Alban in central Mexico, carvings again show distinctively African features and African dancing. There is also a carving of a bearded face with Middle Eastern features, and others that resemble the Sphinx at Giza as well as the Egyptian sun god Ra.[19] Carvings

Corn in Egypt and Egyptians in the Americas

and murals in ancient Egyptian temples show that Egyptians rarely had much facial hair on the chin, and the Nubians none. However, the Pharaohs are often shown wearing a ceremonial "false beard" as a symbol of wisdom and maturity. This sort of beard appears on a sculpture from Kush, dated about 1200 BCE. It is at or about this period, from 1500 to 1000 BCE, that we find Nubians sculpted in the arts of ancient Mexico. What is bizarre is that one of these Olmec sculptures shows the same sort of distinctive woven beard that is on the carving from Kush (ancient Nubia).[20]

Two sets of petroglyphs on cave walls deep in the heartland of the USA indicate a possible Egyptian origin. They were first fully described in 1993; one is situated in Oklahoma and the other at Rochester Creek in central Utah. If they do prove to be of genuine ancient Egyptian origin, this will indicate a far deeper penetration of America by the Egyptians than has previously been imagined.[21] Archaeologist and epigrapher Gloria Farley suggested a possible Egyptian link for the Oklahoma site when she identified a doglike figure in one of the caves as that of Anubis.[22] Certain inscriptions indicate that the site is equinoctial. Interactions with the sun have indeed been recorded by Rollin Gillespie, Phil Leonard, William McGlone, and Jon Polansky. The discovery was reported in the TV documentary *History on the Rocks* that was produced by Scott Monahan of Denver, Colorado.[23] Near Anubis in the second cave is a carving of a woman displaying her birth canal, which was identified as a *sheela-na-gig* by Farley. *Sheela-na-gigs* are crude medieval carvings of female genitalia found frequently in medieval churches and cathedrals in Europe as well as numerous sites in Scotland. The possibility of an Egyptian/Phoenician source for this figure has been clearly indicated by two similar depictions discovered on the Phoenician coast, dating to the first millennium BCE.[24] Stern described these in 1989.

There are further similarities between these North American petroglyphs and ancient Egyptian custom and belief that have been reported by archaeologist Phil Leonard during investigations at Rochester Creek. Leonard and a colleague attempted to interpret one the Rochester Creek panels by using the meanings assigned to the figures in Egyptian iconography. These depict the classic Egyptian story of the soul's journey after death, with all its attendant perils, before it reaches its final destination. A large rainbowlike arch frames the right side of the main panel. Beneath the arch is a female figure exposing her birth canal, which frames a light-colored circle. Immediately under the carving is a reclining ithyphallic male figure. In Egyptian beliefs, the goddess Nut gives birth to the Sun each morning, and she is frequently shown giving birth with her consort, Geb, reclining beneath her. Two beetles shown within the area are framed by the arch, and in Egyptian iconography, the dung beetle, or scarab, is intimately associated with the rising sun. A serpent under the left end of the arch clearly portrays an Egyptian cobra; also shown are hippopotamus-like creatures, crocodiles, and a dog baring its teeth and tongue. In Egyptian tradition, the soul on its final journey is subjected to attack by a strange creature that is known as "the Devourer of the Unjust." This creature is part crocodile and part hippopotamus. There are numerous other figures of possible Egyptian origin, and David Kelley, after a personal examination of the site, claims that the "mere presence of a possible hippo is highly suggestive of a tradition originating entirely outside this continent."[25] Drawings of the inscriptions, along with their Egyptian suggestions, were forwarded to a senior Egyptologist, Professor J. Gwyn Griffiths of the University College of Swansea in Wales. He made the following comment:

> Several of the individual units and groups are in my view attractively explained by these suggestions. The central arch seems to be a vault of heaven (rather than a celestial river), but this supports the idea that the daily birth and course of the sun is depicted.[26]

We agree with William McGlone, Phil Leonard, James Guthrie, and Jim Whittall that the startling similarities between ancient Egyptian iconography and the petroglyphs at this site cannot be honestly or accurately described by the term *Amerindian rock art*.[27] A distinct and identifiable Egyptian influence is present in these glyphs. Open-minded and meticulous investigations of sites such as these are essential. They cannot be simply dismissed without further analysis, especially as the former president of the New World Foundation, Thomas Stuart Ferguson, has reported that seals marked with Egyptian hieroglyphs have been discovered in southern Mexico at Chiapa de Corzo.[28]

A further bizarre anomaly that proves beyond all doubt that ancient Egyptians visited America was revealed to my co-author Wallace-Murphy as the result of a visit to the Island of Orkney in the first few days of September 1997. He was there as one of the speakers at the Sinclair Symposium, a convention convened to discuss Sinclair family history and the pre-Columbian voyage to America made by Nicolo Zeno and Earl Henry St. Clair of Orkney over a century before Columbus made his supposed "voyage of discovery."

It is worthwhile noting here that *St. Clair* and *Sinclair* have a common origin point, in recent times the style *Sinclair* being the more common. The surname originates from a town known as St. Clair-sur-Epte, near Paris, France. This name is shortened in French to *de Sancto Claro* and in Latin, *Sanctus Clarus*, meaning something like "Holy Light." The family were granted land in this area following a treaty signed there in 911 between Rollo (Norse) and Charles (King of the Franks). The descendants of Rollo took the surname St. Clair and fought alongside William the Conqueror at Hastings. Other members of the family settled in Scotland, such as William "the Seemly" St. Clair, who joined the court of Malcolm Canmore, who granted lands at Rosslyn. The surname corrupted to Sinclair from St. Clair over time.

Contributors to the symposium were invited to the local Masonic lodge as a treat and shown their most treasured artifact, the Kirkwall Scroll. The scroll is nearly 18.5 feet long and nearly 6 feet wide. It is composed of three panels—a wide central one flanked by two side panels—and is decorated with Masonic symbols, Hebrew script, and hieroglyphics. When the master of the lodge was asked about the meaning of the hieroglyphics, he could not answer. At this point, one of the party, Dr. Peter Christmas of the Mi'kmaq people of Nova Scotia, stepped up and gave an accurate rendition of the message in hieroglyphics. Afterward my coauthor asked him how long he had studied Egyptology; Dr. Christmas said he never had done so. Inevitably, Wallace-Murphy then asked him how he came to read hieroglyphics. His answer was surprising; Dr. Christmas said that his people had been using them to record important aspects of their history for centuries. Much later Wallace-Murphy discovered a book of some 459 pages written by a catholic priest, Fr. Pierre Maillard, which, in hieroglyphics, recorded the ritual of the Catholic mass, some psalms, and a few items of Catholic doctrine. This book was published in the mid-eighteenth century. Fr. Maillard died in 1762—some sixty-one years before Champollion deciphered the Rosetta Stone and revealed the true worth of hieroglyphics to the world. Long before this pivotal event, the native people of present-day Nova Scotia had been using ancient Egyptian hiero-glyphics fluently and accurately. The imponderable question now arises: Which Egyptian expedition to the Americas was responsible for teaching these people that complex script?

In one of his many books on early voyages to America, Gunnar Thompson mentioned that in 1545, the Archbishop of Brazil astonished Vatican officials when he reported that Egyptian hieroglyphics had been found on ancient ruins near the Atlantic coast. One archaeologist, Carl Stolp, found a lengthy inscription in southern Chile; a stone carving of a griffin-sphinx was found near Cuzco in Peru. Mexican archaeologist Miguel Gonzalez excavated two Egyptian statuettes of the goddess Isis and an unknown pharaoh near San Salvador in 1914. In 1940, Mexican historian Mariano Cuevas reported in his *Historia de la Nacion Mexicana* that "it is a real possibility that Egyptians lived in this ancient city or that it was an Egyptian colony. Their influence in our country (Mexico) could have resulted from immigration—if not by Egyptians, then by peoples in contact with Egypt."[29]

Other scientific clues for sustained Egyptian contact with the Americas have been discovered in Europe, which indicates the motives for these voyages—namely trade. In 1976, Dr. Michelle Lascot of the National History Museum in Paris examined the wrappings of the mummy of the Egyptian Pharaoh Ramses II (c. 1303—1213 BCE) to determine the reason for the degeneration in its condition and was looking for bacterial or viral causes. To her consternation, she found that she was looking at shreds of tobacco.[30] Her discovery caused considerable controversy. When she continued her examination deep inside the mummy itself, she again found

Corn in Egypt and Egyptians in the Americas

she was looking at more shreds of tobacco.[31] As the mummification process based on these procedures was long-standing, sustained trade must have taken place with the American continent, for at that time, this particular type of tobacco was indigenous to America and did not occur elsewhere. The trading implications of these factors were, of course, simply ignored, as they were too uncomfortable for the academic community to contemplate.

Then in 1992, several discoveries were made by the German toxicologist Svetlana Balabanova in the course of her forensic examination of nine Egyptian mummies belonging to the Munich Museum. Taking samples from hair, bone, skin tissue, head, and abdominal muscles, she found a high level of drugs. All nine samples showed traces of hashish—not surprisingly, as this was common in Egypt. Her other findings were so startling that she immediately took steps to have them independently verified by three other laboratories. Eight of the mummies displayed clear evidence of nicotine usage and, the most bizarre result of all, each of the nine clearly demonstrated traces of the active alkaloid of the coca plant—cocaine.[32] The most probable source of the nicotine contamination was explained by ethnobotanist Dr. Michael Carmichael, during The Alternative Egypt Conference in London, as "arising from the Egyptians" and their use of mood-altering drugs derived from mandrake or nightshades that were in common use in that era. The use of the coca plant as a drug, however, has been proven in ancient Peru circa 2500 BCE but was apparently unknown on the other side of the Atlantic until the mid-nineteenth century. Dr. Balabanova is an expert witness whose evidence, in her capacity as a toxicologist, is accepted without question in the courts of Germany, so her methodology is beyond question. Since 1992, further tests have been done on over 3,000 preserved bodies, and a high number of them have proved positive for the presence of nicotine and cocaine.[33] These results were considered so perverse that, of course, they had to be independently verified.

In 1966, Professor Rosalie David of Manchester University in England was asked by a leading TV company to conduct similar tests on mummies kept in her own department of Egyptology. The skeptical David found, to her surprise, that three of the mummies she examined tested positive for nicotine, but all her samples were negative for cocaine.[34] Since then, albeit begrudgingly, scientists have been forced to consider seriously what, to them, was the least likely but is now the only possible conclusion: sustained and prolonged trade had taken place between Egypt and the Americas. While it is possible that tobacco could, theoretically at least, have been cultivated in Africa after its importation from America, no such case can be made for cocaine. Therefore, the only reasonable explanation for this high level of usage must be sustained trade between Egypt and the American continent and that these German tests may simply reflect the fact that the Native Americans were happy to trade cocaine and tobacco for bronze and iron tools. Thus, we can see from the vast array of evidence that can be found on both sides of the Atlantic that ancient Egyptians had prolonged and repeated contact with the Americas over 2,500 years before Christopher Columbus made his well-publicized voyage in 1492.

CHAPTER 3

Classical Greece and the Roman Empire

As for me, I am tormented with an everlasting itch for things remote. I love to sail forbidden seas, and land on barbarous coasts.

—Herman Melville

The ancient Greeks inhabited a series of city-states that, as often as not, were at war with each other. They had considerable skill as boatbuilders, and their ships traded throughout the Mediterranean Sea. Their combined maritime power was considerable; for example, they defeated the Persian fleet at the Battle of Salamis in 480 BCE. They not only built powerful warships propelled by oars but also had a considerable number of large merchant sailing vessels of about 115 feet in length. By the middle of the third century BCE, the Greeks were building grain freighters of 1,900 tons burden, ships that were ten times the size of Columbus's Santa Maria and at least twice the size of the largest galleon used on Spanish voyages to and from the New World.[1]

Insofar as it can be established, the various Greek written sources describing cross-Atlantic travel were almost certainly based on secondhand knowledge derived from Phoenician or Egyptian sources. The Phoenicians and their Carthaginian descendants controlled access to the Atlantic and blocked or discouraged anyone seeking to venture onto their trade routes. Thus, until the fall of Carthage in 146 BCE, their near monopoly continued unchecked. However, with the blockade lifted, the Romans soon began to venture forth upon the Atlantic Ocean.

The range and size of Roman ships often surprise people. Many of their cargo vessels were also considerably bigger than the ships used by Columbus in 1492. On the low end there were ships designed for the grain trade, which carried 10,000 *modii* of grain, a little over 75 tons; they were the workhorses of the fleet, running regular routes to nearby provinces. Transporting the grain that government contracts provided for, the ship owners were also provided with a steady source of income as their vessels traced and retraced the same path back and forth between Rome, Sicily, Alexandria, and the rest of the republic and empire. Larger ships were used extensively for the olive oil trade (especially around the province of Hispania Baetica in southern Spain) and were measured by the number of amphorae they could hold. A 3,000-amphorae vessel had almost three times the capacity of the smaller ships. The size of these ships is confirmed by numerous underwater archaeological examinations of shipwrecks and written accounts of the time.[2] Small- and medium-sized ships also carried general merchandise such as metal ores, a variety of raw materials, spices, silk, and other trade goods. For instance, in the first century CE, 120 ships a year set sail for India from the Red Sea ports of Berenike and Myos Hormos.[3] Their return cargo consisted of pepper that was moved by barge to Alexandria and then shipped to Rome.

The Roman fleet also had higher tonnage vessels. The hull of the ship at Madrague de Giens, a wreck off the coast of Gaul in the first century BCE, was 130 feet long and had an estimated capacity of 440 tons. In the early years of the Roman Empire, the *muriophorio*, 10,000-amphorae carriers carrying 550 tons, were the largest ships afloat; the grain trade utilized some 50,000 *modii* vessels that hauled 365 tons. The size and capacity of these ships were not exceeded in the Mediterranean until the sixteenth century. The Roman world saw a few ships even larger than these—the carrier that Caligula built to transport an obelisk from Egypt to Rome had a capacity of 1,450 tons. Various emperors and their consorts, Cleopatra among them, built barge-like floating palaces, and although designed for limited use in safe waters, some of these ships were nearly 250 feet in length. Thus, Roman ships considerably larger than Columbus's flagship, the Santa Maria, were common by the time of Jesus. Lionel Casson, a historian who specialized in ancient shipping, confirmed that the Romans had cargo carriers of about 340 tons burden and grain ships of 1,200 tons. The cargo ships were constructed of pine, fir, or cedar, and their hulls were often clad with sheets of lead below the waterline, with a layer of tarred fabric sandwiched between the lead and the wooden hull. The sails were made of linen and cordage of flax, hemp, twisted papyrus, or sometimes leather.

In 150 BCE the Roman historian Pausanias described a group of islands west of the Atlantic inhabited by people whose hair was "like that of a horse." Roman consul Metellus Celer recorded that when he was officiating in Gaul in 62 BCE, the king of a neighboring province brought him several exotic-looking men with different skins and black hair. He was informed that they had been blown across the Atlantic in a large wooden canoe and cast up on the coast. Thus, there is little doubt that the Romans were aware of land on the other side of the ocean.[4] This is borne out by references in a variety of classical texts. Lands situated beyond the Pillars of Hercules are mentioned by Aristotle, or one of his pupils,[5] Plato,[6] Diodorus Siculus,[7] Theopompus of Chios,[8] Plutarch,[9] Strabo,[10] and Eratosthenes of Cyrene.[11] While many of these may well be secondhand comments, as mentioned earlier, others obviously speak from direct observation and experience:

> The impassable farther bounds of Ocean not only has no one attempted to describe, but no man has been allowed to reach; for the reason of obstructing seaweed and the failing of winds, it is plainly inaccessible. . . . The same ocean has in its western region certain islands known to almost everyone by reason of the great number of those who journey to and fro.[12]

Plato wrote that "far to the west of the British Isles were other islands beyond which, at the edge of the sea, stretched a great continent."[13] In the ruins of Pompeii, murals contain accurate portrayals of two indigenous American plants that have been verified by botanists: the pineapple and soursop.[14] These mosaic murals in Pompeii have been dated to the first century CE and also include New World pineapples. Even that one-time critic of early voyages, the plant taxonomist Elmer Drew Merrill, has accepted this as proof of early contact between Europe and America. Archaeologists have also removed maize kernels from a Roman grain silo in Spain, and a Roman book of plants includes New World pumpkins.[15]

While we should emphasize that the following is speculation, the disappearance of the herb, contraceptive, and aphrodisiac silphium might also provide another economic reason for the desire for Roman trade further afield. Silphium, which is the speculated origin of the heart shape that is synonymous with love, from its heart-shaped seeds, was found only in Cyrenaica in modern-day Libya. The plant, which is described as having military and culinary uses, including that of avoiding scurvy, is recorded as having been lost during the time of Nero.[16] Despite this, similarly described plants appear abundantly over the prairies of North America and were used by some native tribes for a similar purpose.[17] For a plant that was described by Pliny as "being worth its weight in silver," could this provide an economic motive for potential Roman trade in the Americas? If we are to further the argument for some form of continuous trade, it is worthwhile noting the length of the mare nostrum (Mediterranean Sea), whose entire shores Rome occupied. From end to end, the Mediterranean spans from the Strait of Gibraltar to the Gulf of İskenderun and measures around 2,500 miles. The Roman Empire was roughly, in terms of travel, 4 months long and wide. This said, the shortest distance between Africa, in which Rome had provinces, and South America is around 1,600 miles. Could Rome or others have mastered this comparatively shorter transatlantic voyage?

The evidence of Roman contact with the New World that can be found on the American side of the pond is quite amazing. One earlier commentator, Marineus Siculus, recounts in his *Chronicle of Spaine* written in the sixteenth century that a certain quantity of Roman gold coins were discovered in a gold mine in America:

> [C]ertaine pieces of money engraved with the image of Augustus Caesar: which pieces were sent to the Pope for a testomonie of the matter, by John Rufus, Archbishop of Consentium.[18]

Presumably, these coins still languish somewhere in the Vatican. One indisputably Roman artifact, a terra-cotta head found by a reputable archaeologist during a properly supervised and recorded dig in Mexico, is dated to the second century CE. The archaeologist, José García Payón of Mexico's National Museum, made the discovery in 1933. It was found under a cement floor that was dated to the eleventh century CE, and, therefore, the terra-cotta head cannot be described as a colonial import.[19] Because of the circumstances of the find (buried under datable intact flooring), which occurred in the course of a museum-sponsored excavation, there can be no argument whatsoever about its authenticity. Yet this proof of Roman contact with Central America has been greeted with deafening silence by the academic establishment in the United States.[20] Writing in the early 1800s, John Haywood, chief justice of the Supreme Court of Tennessee, stated that many Roman coins were found in Tennessee and adjacent states.[21] More recently, Canaanite coins of the Bar Kokhba Revolt (132–135 CE) have been found by farmers around Louisville, Hopkinsville, and Clay City, Kentucky.[22]

In the mid-twentieth century, many ancient Roman artifacts were excavated from a variety of pre-Columbian sites in Central and South America. Dozens of classical Greco-Roman terra-cotta oil lamps were uncovered in northern Peru in pre-Inca tombs. A most compelling indication of Roman contact with the New World was found in 1961 when Dr. García Payón of the University of Xalapa discovered a hoard of Roman jewelry in six graves near Mexico City. Dr. Robert von Heine-Geldern of the University of Vienna and Professor Hans Boehringer of the German Institute of Archaeology identified them as originating in the second century BCE. Scientific dating of the bones and other material found in association with the jewelry indicates that the burials themselves took place no later than 100 BCE. A hoard of several hundred Roman coins was dug up near the coast in Venezuela, the most recent of which was dated to 350 AD.[23] Earlier, in the Introduction, I (Martin) mentioned the bronze cup found by James Howe near the banks of the Roanoke River. This fascinating cup is identical to one found in Pompeii, which is indisputably dated as being over 2,000 years old.[24]

Several Roman shipwrecks have been located off the coast of the Americas, in the waters of the United States, Honduras, and Brazil. Clearly identifiable artifacts have been recovered from many of them, principally amphorae, or ceramic wine casks. Two amphorae were found in Castings Bay, Maine, in 1971 by a scuba diver at a depth of 12 meters. Colleagues at the Early Sites Research Society in Massachusetts identified them as being of Iberian/Roman manufacture of the first century CE. Another was discovered near the shoreline of Jonesboro, Maine.[25] In 1972, large quantities of amphorae were discovered at the bottom of the Caribbean Sea off the coast of Honduras. Scholars who examined them identified them as originating in North African ports and applied for a permit to do a proper excavation of the wreck. Honduran government officials denied this responsible and legitimate request because "they feared further investigation might compromise the glory of Columbus."[26]

Amphorae of North African manufacture seem oddly destined to end up off the coast of the Americas. In 1976, a Brazilian diver, Roberto Teixeria, found several on the seabed near Rio de Janeiro. Following his initial discovery, more were recovered, including the discovery of a shipwreck of potential Roman origin. As a result, the marine archaeologist Robert Marx inspected the shipwreck. He passed some of the amphorae on to Professor Elizabeth Will of the Department of Classical Greek History at the University of Massachusetts, who identified them as Moroccan. She was able to narrow their manufacture down to the Mediterranean port of Zillis and dated them to the third century CE. Marx recovered several thousand pottery fragments from the wreck before he was denied a permit for further excavation. This time, it is not "pro-Columbian" bias we have to thank for this obstruction; the Brazilian authorities were concerned that any further evidence of ancient Roman voyages would diminish the fame of the "official discoverer of Brazil," Pedro Álvares Cabral.[27]

Marx was no fool, and he had hit the brick wall of denial many times before. When he first examined the original amphorae found near Rio, which were at that time in the custody of the director of IPHAN, the Brazilian Historical and Artistic Institute of Rio de Janeiro, he arranged for them to also be examined, one by the Naval Oceanographic Institute in Rio and the other by the Oceanographic Institute of Rio Grande. Their examinations concluded that the marine growth on the amphorae was not from the Mediterranean but from the Bay of Guanabara, that there was no underlying growth, and that it had taken many hundreds of years to grow. Dr. Eliézer de Carvalho of the Oceanographic Institute of Rio Grande had carbon dating done on the marine growth, which indicated that it was some 2,000 years old, plus or minus 140 years. One IPHAN archaeologist sent one shred to the Institute of Archaeology at the University of London for thermoluminescence testing, which gave a result of 2,000 years plus or minus a century. So, these amphorae had been lying on the seabed near Rio for 2,000 years.[28]

After refusing Robert Marx a permit for further excavation, the Brazilian authorities sought to place this evidence permanently beyond reach; they arranged for a dredger full of mud and silt to cover the wreck and prevent any further examination of it in the future or, as their official announcement put it, "to prevent anyone plundering the site."[29]

CHAPTER 4

The Celts

We are like dwarfs on the shoulders of giants, so that
we can see more than they, and things at a greater
distance, not by virtue of any sharpness of sight on
our part, or any physical distinction, but because we
are carried high and raised up by their giant size.

—BERNARD OF CHARTRES

I (Wallace-Murphy) once saw a bumper sticker that proclaimed "God only invented alcohol to prevent the Irish from taking over the world." It is a somewhat sardonic theory that celebrates two indisputable facts about my fellow countrymen: they tend to drink rather a lot, and they are spread right across the globe. People tend to blame the Irish habit of emigration on the English occupation, but this has not always been the primary cause. The Irish were traveling and exploring for many centuries before the English invasion by Strongbow and his henchmen in 1170 CE. Nomadic by nature and intent, inspired Irish Celtic monks traveled across the sea and evangelized much of Western Europe.[1]

Some fifty years after the death of the Cumbrian St. Patrick on March 17, 461 CE, another Celtic saint continued the work of converting pagans to Christianity. St. Brendan the Navigator, who was born near Tralee in 484 CE, traveled tirelessly to evangelize following his ordination at the age of twenty-eight years. He frequently crossed the sea to spread the Gospel not only throughout Ireland but also in Scotland, Wales, and the north of France.

According to one 1,500-year-old Irish tale, St. Brendan embarked on an epic journey at the great old age of ninety-three. According to the story, St. Barinthus told St. Brendan that he had just returned from a visit to "Paradise," a land that lurked far beyond the horizon. For forty days St. Brendan fasted and prayed atop a mountain on the rugged Dingle Peninsula. The nonagenarian eyed the crashing waves of the Atlantic Ocean for some time before deciding to go in pursuit of this fabled Garden of Eden. He crafted a traditional Irish currach, an open boat with leather skins stretched over the vessel's wooden frame and propelled by oars and square sails. Along with a crew of between 18 and 150, according to the differing accounts, the saint sailed off into the Atlantic. The story recounts that St. Brendan encountered towering crystal pillars afloat in the oceans, landed on an island with sheep the size of oxen, encountered giants who pelted the ship with fireballs that smelled like rotten eggs, and met with talking birds that sang psalms. Eventually, the boat drifted through a fog and landed in a place lush with vegetation, fragrant with flowers, and abounding in fruit and colorful stones. They called this land "Paradise," and it was also identified with the "Fortunate Isles" of the ancients. After the men stayed for forty days, an angel told them to return home. Back in Ireland, pilgrims who heard this sensational story flocked to see the elderly monk in County Kerry until his death in 577 CE.

As with so many other "saints," the line between the history and legend surrounding St. Brendan has been blurred. The account of his voyage was transmitted orally for generations until it was finally put on paper. Three versions of this legend are recorded. Two are from the eighth century: the *Vita Brendani* (the Life of Brendan) and the *Navigato Sancti Brendani* (the Voyage of St. Brendan). A third version is to be found in the twelfth-century work *The Book of Lismore*. In the eighth-century versions, he is described as traveling in a currach accompanied by between eighteen and sixty monks. In the twelfth-century version, he sailed in a wooden craft manned by sixty monks.[2] No archaeological evidence exists to support these legends, with the possible exception of a stone beehive hut at Upton, Massachusetts, that is similar to monks' cells found on the Blasket Isles off the coast of southwestern Ireland.[3] These books and their contents became so widely known that cartographers began to include "Paradise," recorded as "St. Brendan's Island," on maps. It is claimed that Christopher Columbus was aware of the elusive island—which was drawn on a variety of places on maps from the southwest of Ireland to near the Canary Islands off the African coast—as he embarked on his own voyage in 1492.

The St. Brendan legend describes "Paradise" as being over ten times the size of Ireland. One Celtic clan, the Fomorians, are believed to have sought refuge there after a defeat in battle. Indeed, as other legends recount, several Irish heroes are said to have sailed west to an idyllic land called Mag Mell, or *Tir na nÓg*.[4] Moreover, legends of transatlantic Celtic travel are not restricted to the Land of Saints and Scholars. The folk traditions of some Native American people tend to confirm some of their blarneying blather. One Abenaki researcher, Bernard Assiniwi, recounts that he heard this story from a native elder:

> Our chiefs speak of strangers who came to us by boat from the sea about two thousand years ago. They established their colonies on our territory trying to take us by force. But, after they had destroyed their vessels, our Algonquin fathers convinced them to live among us. They called themselves "Kelts."[5]

Then, in 1976, the St. Brendan legend received an unexpected boost. Just as Thor Heyerdahl's epic voyages proved the feasibility of early transatlantic and transpacific voyages under extremely primitive conditions, Tim Severin's 1976 voyage in which he recreated the St. Brendan story in a currach—a wooden-framed canvas-covered boat—was a vibrant proof of the viability of St. Brendan's voyage as told in that ancient legend. While many authors have commented on the startling similarity in the descriptions made about aspects of the New World in classical texts and in the Celtic legends, this similarity should be treated with considerable caution. The explanation of these similarities is far more prosaic.

In direct contrast to the prevailing practices in the Catholic Church, Celtic Christianity was characterized by its spiritual purity and simplicity. Priests in the Celtic Church were encouraged to marry, and the priesthood was, like that in the early Jerusalem Church, a hereditary office.[6] No images of the crucifixion were allowed, and Celtic priests refused to practice infant baptism.[7] Unlike the emerging Catholic Church, the Celtic Church resolutely rejected all the trappings and benefits of temporal power and also refused to recognize the supremacy of the Catholic pope. The simplicity and humility of the Celtic priests posed a direct challenge to the pomp and circumstance of the comfortable and powerful priesthood in the rest of Europe. This situation was given force and point, as the result of the enormous cultural dynamism possessed by the Celtic mystics and monks whose artwork, scholarship, and scriptural learning were exemplary. Thomas Fuller, the seventeenth-century historian, described the Celtic missionaries who traversed all of Europe, from Scandinavia in the north to Switzerland in the east, as "the wandering scholars." Another point that differentiates them from their Catholic counterparts was their knowledge of the Greek and Latin classics that their Catholic colleagues condemned as "pagan." Such was the quality and range of their classical learning that Professor Heinrich Zimmer claims that "it is almost a truism to state that whoever knew Greek in the days of Charles the Bald (ninth century CE) was an Irishman or had been taught by an Irishman."[8] Thus, in an era when illiteracy was the rule rather than the exception, knowledge of the Greek and Latin classical authors was common among the scholars of Ireland. This may well explain the startling similarity between the comments of classical authors of antiquity and Irish commentators about lands across the Atlantic.

Several authors have tried to convince the general public of the possibility of some degree of truth behind the fascinating stories of Celtic transatlantic exploration, such as William B. Goodwin, whose work *The Ruins of Great Ireland in New England* tells us more about the author's obsession than it does of factual history. Professor Barry Fell's work *America BC*, while somewhat flawed, deserves far better study than the blanket condemnation it has received to date. While Fell may well be accused of "over-egging the pudding" in many respects, his discoveries and theories merit far more serious attention than they have received to date.

Wallace-Murphy, as an Irishman, would have loved to be able to claim that his ancestors had crossed the Atlantic centuries before Columbus, but alas neither of us can. St. Brendan and all the other Irish claimants to pre-Columbian American exploration still remain matters of legend, and *not* of fact. Who knows what may emerge in the way of hard evidence in the future, but that is how the matter stands at the moment of writing.

The Welsh Traditions

Our romantic fellow countrymen in Ireland are not the only Celts whose culture records tales of transatlantic voyages and settlements. Indeed, as my fellow author, Wallace-Murphy, points out, Cumbrians, Britons, and the larger Celtic community may have had some claim also. The Welsh, for example, claim that Prince Madoc ab Owain Gwynedd was the true discoverer of America.[9] According to the Welsh legend, Madoc is reputed to have sent three expeditions across the ocean: "the first to reconnoitre the ocean passage, the second to scout for suitable land and the third comprising a fleet of ten ships carrying settlers, cattle and farm animals."[10] The legend of Madoc's voyage was recorded by Caradoc of Llancarfan in *Historia Cambria*, which was translated into English in 1584 to substantiate Tudor England's claim to have settled North America. Yet another account can be found in volume 4 of *Originibus Americanus*, published in The Hague in 1652, which claims

> Madoc, a prince of Cambria, with some of his nation, discovered and settled some lands in the west, and that his name and his memory are still retained among the people there scarcely any doubt remains.[11]

Although the voyages of both St. Brendan and Madoc still are classed as legendary, it is a matter of record that the Spanish reported finding ancient stone forts in Florida and attributed their origins to ancient Welsh settlers.[12] One Shawnee chief, Black Hoof, claimed that there was an ancient story that spoke of a white race in Florida long before the Spanish arrived. Furthermore, in the early years of colonial settlement, there were numerous unsubstantiated tales of Welsh-speaking Native Americans in circulation. One Native American tribe, the Mandans of North Dakota, was described as "white men in red men's dress who understand Welsh."[13] Sadly, the Mandan people can no longer be consulted, as due to the generous gift of blankets deliberately infected with smallpox, 90 percent of their tribe were killed.

There are other more circumstantial indications of possible Celtic settlements in the Americas: the American antiquarian Arlington Mallery claimed that many of the sites he had visited in the Eastern United States during the 1940s were iron-smelting furnaces of Celtic origin, another matter that demands serious study. In 1986, Joseph Gardner and his team found what they believed to be substantiation of the Welsh legends of Old Stone Fort near Chattanooga, Tennessee; DeSoto Falls, Alabama; and Fort Mountain, Georgia. In Mallery's view, these forts were not of Native American construction but nonetheless apparently dated from the twelfth century. The Tennessee site, in particular, bore a close resemblance to medieval forts found in Wales. While no irrefutable evidence of Celtic habitation has been found in the Americas, it has, nonetheless, been clearly established that the Celts reached Greenland. In that land it was found that later visitors, namely the Vikings, erected their dwellings on clearly Celtic foundations.[14]

Is truth stranger than fiction? Of course, it is; it always has been. Queen Elizabeth I was persuaded by her advisors that this was so, and the alleged "Prince Madoc Welsh discovery of America" was put forward as somehow giving England a prior claim in the political wrangles over first rights in carving up the New World. Up to that point, no one had even thought to investigate the British records. Caradoc of Llancarfan wrote about Madoc's voyage in the 1140s. The information was made available to historian

Richard Hakluyt, who wrongly dated the voyages to around 1170, which, of course, would be impossible, as Caradoc of Llancarfan could not have recorded voyages that took place fourteen years after he died! William Fleming, of Flemingston, near Cardiff, wrote poetry on the subject before Caradoc died, so the idea of voyages being made in 1170 becomes even weaker. In 1625, the Archbishop of Canterbury wrote a world history stating that a Welsh prince had discovered America and that "King Arthur knew of it." In essence, the anecdote suggests a voyage in the seventh century by Arthur II, the son of King Meurig, who was a direct male descendant of Arthur I, who could have been the sixth-century Arthur of legend and so on and so on. These stories are fascinating, romantic, and absolutely unproven, so the Welsh claims to early transatlantic exploration are, like their Irish counterparts, still classified as "the stuff of legend."

CHAPTER 5

The Viking Voyages: Myth or Reality?

Wisdom is welcome wherever it comes from.

—The Bandamanna Saga

B ias is not restricted to the modern era; it was endemic among the historians of the Dark Ages in Europe. They were all priests who recorded the myths, legends, and history of converted peoples and, in that process, distorted them beyond belief. The bias was sometimes subtle, giving a Christian gloss here and there to pagan legends, adopting local pagan gods and goddesses as Christian saints, but sometimes more brutally, adding this or omitting that to tell a coherent story that reinforced the supremacy of Christianity and the Church. This was the milieu in which the Vikings (perhaps meaning "trader") emerged, and these wild raiders got short shrift from Christian commentators as richly endowed churches and monasteries had become their principal targets—hardly an endearing habit for a Christian chronicler. The Viking raiders were masters of the seas and rivers of Europe, which meant that they could strike almost anywhere and without warning. Above all else, the Vikings were shipbuilders *par excellence*.[1]

The Longship

Without any shadow of doubt, the longship was the supreme achievement of Viking culture. It gave these warriors from the north the means by which raids, trade, and exploration could take place. It was not only the principal means of transport but also a source of marine power and, for leaders and noblemen of note, their final resting place on the road to Valhalla. It was this habit of using longships for the burial of the great and the good that has given historians and archaeologists the means to discover an intimate and detailed knowledge of Viking shipbuilding techniques.

Until fairly recently, the coastline of Oslofjord was adorned by three man-made mounds, one on the eastern shore at Tune and two more to the west at Oseberg and Gokstad.[2] They were all erected over ships. They were excavated in the latter part of the nineteenth century and the beginning of the twentieth. All three ships are now on view at the ship museum on the Island of Bygdøy, only a short boat ride from Oslo itself. The boat at Tune was the first to be excavated in 1867.[3] The second, the largest, which is believed to date from about 900 CE, was excavated at Gokstad in 1880.[4] The third was excavated at Oseberg in 1904.[5] Five more longships in an almost perfect state of preservation were discovered in 1962 at Roskilde Fjord in Denmark.[6] Another was found in 1970. Thus, in the space of a little more than a century, finds have been made that have allowed historians and modern boatbuilders alike to assess Viking shipbuilding techniques with great accuracy and comment upon their seamanship with precision.

The superb find at Gokstad was originally built to sail or be rowed. It is of clinker construction with sixteen rows of planks, each one overlapping the one beneath and caulked with threads of tarred wool.[7] The planking is lashed to the ribs with withies held in cleats, not nailed to them. The ribs are not fastened to the keel, which endows the hull with considerably more flexibility than modern shipbuilding techniques. The fourteenth row of planking is pierced with sixteen oar-holes on each side of the ship. Each of these is furnished with wooden shutters that could be closed when under sail.

The keel is 20.10 meters in length and is cut from a single piece of wood in such a manner as to give it the greatest possible strength with the least possible weight.[8] The height from the keel to the top of the gunnel is 2.02 meters. Length from stem to stern is 23.30 meters, the maximum beam is 5.20 meters, and the weight of the hull fully equipped is estimated at 20.2 metric tons. Lying across the stern was a specially constructed burial chamber in which was found the remains of a Viking chieftain; sadly, his weapons were missing.[9] In 1893 a replica of the Gokstad ship crossed the Atlantic under the command of Captain Magnus Andersen.[10] According to Andersen, the ship's performance was remarkable, and her rudder was a work of genius. In one day, May 15, 1893, she covered 223 nautical miles in twenty-four hours, an hourly average of 9.3 knots, outsailing the steamships of that time. Using ships like this, the Viking raiders became the scourge of the coasts and estuaries of Western Europe. Their potential use of *sólarsteinn* (sunstones) allowed for bearing navigation in an age before the magnetic compass, enabling precision voyages with immense speed.[11] Their exploits became fodder for the Christian scribes as they wrote their distorted versions of history. But what sort of people were the Vikings in reality?

Viking Culture

Certainly, the Vikings were no less cruel than their Christian victims, and perhaps the only difference between them was the Vikings' habit of plundering churches, monasteries, and abbeys. However, this was only one aspect of a multifaceted civilization that, because of its mastery of the sea, was able to exert a truly transformative effect on most of the other cultures it touched. As raiders, traders, mercenary soldiers, and explorers, they displayed considerable acumen. Between the eighth and tenth centuries, they created a series of trading links that spanned the known world. As a result, they were able to bring back to their northern homelands the products and ideas of the entire Mediterranean coast from Byzantium to the Pillars of Hercules. They founded Moscow and traversed the vast lands of Russia by river (the Kievan Rus'), reaching both the Caspian and the Black Seas.[12] Due to population pressures in their homelands, the Vikings became colonizers and settlers in Orkney, Caithness, York, Dublin, and the east coast of Ireland; the south coast of Ireland; northern France; Sicily; Iceland; and Greenland.[13]

Contrary to the rather shallow view of Vikings purveyed by popular mythology, they developed a rich, sophisticated, and complex culture infused with an early form of democracy. The royal rule of the kings of Norway was moderated by a parliament (Þing) of leading nobles.[14] Under their benevolent rule, Scandinavia became a cultural crossroads where ideas that originated in far countries were imported, resynthesized, and re-exported to overseas Viking settlements. The Vikings built in stone at a time when most of the rest of Europe still used wood and wattle. They were superb bridge builders. Viking craftsmen created jewelry that is still a source of wonder and delight to archaeologists and historians, with vivid examples of this particular art form being seen in the Viking hoard discovered in Ireland in January 2000.

Viking culture was an oral one, and their history, myths, and legends did not achieve literary form until much later, between the twelfth and fourteenth centuries. Thus, the Viking sagas are transcribed from earlier oral traditions and include *The Íslendingabók*, *The Flateyjarbók*, *The Hauksbók*, *The Færeyinga Saga,* and *The Orkneyinga Saga*. At first, they were regarded as mere myths and folklore; however, academic opinion about them has changed dramatically over the last two centuries. Although they are couched in narrative form, they are rich in historical detail that has served as a literary signpost pointing to irrefutable evidence of Viking occupations in Iceland, Greenland, and Newfoundland.[15] The authenticity of the sagas as historical documents is now generally accepted, and the only significant point of difference that arises among scholars is over the exact dating of the events described within them. Even here, the divergence is usually less than two years.

The Sagas

The earliest saga to be written down was the Íslendingabók, which was transcribed by an Icelandic priest known as Ari the Learned, otherwise known as Ari Fróði, between 1122 and 1132.[16] This saga gives an account of both Viking exploration and settlement on the islands and coast of the great northern ocean, and Vinland is mentioned on four occasions. Ari records that when the Vikings settled in Greenland, they found the remains of buildings and stone tools left by previous settlers. In 1991, historian Ian Wilson suggested that these pre-Norse ruins may well have been the remnants of earlier Celts who had inhabited Greenland previously.[17] This has since been confirmed by archaeological investigation. However, Hjalmar Holand claims that the earliest mention of Vinland is to be found on a runic inscription on a stone discovered in Norway and not in the sagas.[18]

It is easy to get confused when first studying the Vinland story, as there are two different accounts, each of which is seemingly authoritative. One is the *Flateyjarbók*, written in Old Icelandic in the late 1300s, which was given to the King of Denmark in 1647 by a Mr. Hakonarson.[19] The other, and perhaps the earlier source, is the *Hauksbók* written by Hauk Erlendsson, who died in 1334 and who was a direct descendant of Thorfinn Karlsefni, and this work contains "Karlsefni's saga."[20] Many scholars believe that the *Flateyjarbók* comes from a more direct Greenland source, and thus, it is often referred to as "The Greenland Saga."[21] The tone and nature of these two works are very different: the *Hauksbók* is a richly embroidered hagiography of Karlsefni, whereas the *Flateyjarbók* is written in a spare and direct narrative form, containing accurate sailing directions.[22]

Viking Exploration of the North Atlantic

The Vikings were motivated by two principal aims: the scarcity of land in Scandinavia and greed for plunder as well as lands to settle. Iceland was discovered by accident when Garðar Svarvasson was blown off course sailing from Norway to the Hebrides in 861.[23] The first Viking settlers arrived some nine years later and found that Celtic monks from Ireland were already living there. These monks were somewhat underwhelmed with the arrival of the Vikings and left with great haste, leaving behind "bells, books and croziers," as recorded in the *Landnámabók*. However, Iceland's main claim to fame in Viking history is as the birthplace of

Eiríkur hinn Rauði, better known to us today as Erik the Red. In 982 he set sail westward and made his first landfall in Greenland at a place that was later called Blacksark. Sailing southward, he was looking for pastureland suitable for settlement. Erik spent the winter on the island of Eriskay in the Briedifjord.[24] When the snows melted, he sailed on to Tunugdliarfik, where, on the inland side, he found the site he chose for his farm. During the summer, he continued his exploration naming every island, fjord, and headland as he went. Despite all rumors to the contrary, he did not name this country; it had already been referred to as Greenland, a place to be administered, by the Archbishop of Hamburg in 831.[25] By the summer of 986, Erik sailed for Greenland with a fleet of thirty-five ships and over 1,000 people; however, a storm scattered the fleet, and only fourteen ships and 400 people eventually made landfall.[26] Sometime later, Bjarni Herjulfsson set sail from Iceland to join the settlement in Greenland. His ship was blown off course in a storm, and he passed previously unknown lands—some were well wooded with low hills and no mountains. When he finally arrived in Greenland, he described his adventures in such a manner that others could locate the lands he had seen.[27]

The early twentieth-century historian Frederick Pohl plotted Bjarni's course on a map, and in line with Bjarni's description of his first landfall, he concluded that this was at Cape Cod, which fits the Viking's description.[28] The saga recounts that Bjarni then sailed out of sight of land for two days until he came to a well-wooded flat country that both Pohl and Hjalmar Holand agree was present-day Nova Scotia.[29] The third sighting of land was, most probably, Newfoundland, where again the topography matches the description in the saga.

Erik the Red's colony in Greenland survived for several centuries.[30] Eventually, it grew to support sixteen parish churches, a cathedral, a monastery, and a nunnery. Some thirteen years after the foundation of the colony, Erik sent his son, Leif Eriksson, to Norway. On arrival, Leif was evangelized by King Olaf Tryggvason by being requested to make a simple choice—Christianity or a swim in a vat of boiling oil. Given the options, it should be of no surprise that he chose Christianity.[31] After wintering in present-day Trondheim, Leif returned home under a royal command to convert his people. They all converted, with one notable exception—his father, Erik the Red.[32]

Leif set out to explore the lands that Bjarni had seen and made his first landfall at the mountainous island that Bjarni had described. He found it and set foot on an area of flat rock—that Leif called Helluland.[33] Sailing onward they then landed at the second place Bjarni had seen, near some woods fringed with white sand. At this point the land sloped gently down toward the sea, and Leif named this country Markland—the Land of Forests.[34] Detecting a change in wind direction and strength, Leif and his men then sailed southwest for two days, about 300 miles travel in a long-ship, before they made landfall again. This would have placed them in the region of southern New England.[35] They must have thought that they had landed in paradise: the rivers abounded with salmon, the grass was lush and frost-free, and the land was well wooded.[36] The party then built shelters for the winter before dividing into two groups—one to guard their houses, the other to explore the surrounding countryside. The saga goes on to report that one evening a man went missing; when a search party found him, he was in high spirits for he had found grapevines and grapes. It is alleged that on this basis, Leif called this land Vinland, and according to Hjalmar Holand, it was discovered in 1003 CE.[37] After wintering there, Leif and his men sailed home with a boat filled with produce from this new land.

The Voyage of Leif's Brother, Thorwald

When Leif returned to Greenland, his brother, Thorwald, decided to go to Vinland and continue its exploration. This would have been in the year of Leif's return in 1004 CE or, at most, one year later.[38] When his party arrived at the site of Leif's winter quarters, Thorwald also divided his party into two—one part to explore the shore to the west of the settlement,[39] most probably the present-day areas of Block Island Sound and Long Island Sound. The following summer, Thorwald took a small party and sailed eastward, passing Nantucket Sound, and then turned north where gale-force winds blew them ashore on a headland (perhaps Cape Cod?). The keel of their boat was damaged when it was beached, and it took some time to effect repairs. When they took to the sea again, they sailed northward and explored the lands between Vinland and Markland. When they reached a headland with a deep-water anchorage, Thorwald decided that this was where he would make his home.[40]

On making their way back to the boat, Thorwald and his party encountered nine natives and killed eight of them. As a result, they were later attacked by natives in a fleet of canoes and were met with a shower of arrows. There was one casualty—Thorwald, who, knowing he was facing imminent death, ordered his men to bury him at the site he had chosen for his home.[41] After burying Thorwald, the rest of the party returned to Vinland and there cut timber to take back to Greenland.

Thorfinn Karlsefni's Exploration

Thorfinn Karlsefni, a Viking of royal descent and wealthy man in his own right, arrived in Greenland in 1008 or 1009, along with Snorri Thorbrandsson, an old friend of Erik the Red, with a crew of forty men. Soon afterward another ship of about the same size arrived, under the command of Bjarni Grimolfsson and Thorhall Gamalson. Leif invited the leaders and men of both ships to spend the winter as his guests. Later, Thorfinn married Gudrid, a widow who was a ward of Leif Eriksson.[42] During the winter, Thorfinn was brought up to date with the explorations of Vinland, and he determined to sail there and see for himself. He took a large party with him that included residents of Greenland, along with cattle, as they intended to found a permanent settlement there. The *Flateyjarbók* tells how the party sailed on the traditional route to Vinland and stayed there for two years. After being subjected to concerted attacks from natives, Thorfinn decided to return to Greenland. The saga continues by telling of the birth of Thorfinn's son, Snorri, who therefore became the first person of European extraction born in the New World.

There have been many attempts to identify the exact locations of both Vinland and Markland; they have resulted in some consensus with Markland being identified with Nova Scotia and Vinland as somewhere in New England. Leif's original settlement was most likely to have been near Narragansett Bay in the area near present-day Newport, Rhode Island.[43] Records of Viking trade and modern archaeology tend to confirm this, as the archaeologist Helge Ingstad informs us that anthracite coal that originated in Rhode Island was found in Greenland.[44] Leif Eriksson started a trade route when he first brought back timber and grapes from Vinland to Greenland. The manifests of cargoes that were landed in Bergen show that ships from Greenland brought to Europe a variety of valuable furs,[45] including marmot, otter, beaver, wolverine, lynx, sable, and black bear, but none of these were native to Greenland; all were from the New World.

Chasing the Unicorn

The extent to which the Vikings influenced contemporary European culture by way of trade originating in North America should not be understated. One such influence was the curious explosion in depictions of the unicorn in territories visited by the Norse from the beginning of the eleventh century. While the unicorn has been depicted since classical antiquity,[46] the familiar notion of a horselike creature explodes throughout the period of the Norse exploration of the Americas: an animal that can run like a horse, that could fly away (thus requiring additional skill to capture it), and crucially, that had a valuable commodity—ivory. As is the case today, owning a horse, let alone one that could fly, is an expensive business. To the medieval laborer, the upkeep of a horse would have cost the equivalent of one year's salary, and, as such, horse ownership was a luxury afforded to the landed elites. Alongside pack animals, the horse's value was enhanced, as they provided for transport, military service, and rapid delivery of information.

The Norse were noted traders, and while we do not suggest that the unicorn existed, the notion of unicorn ivory did exist in the medieval period. Several items, including bishops' croziers and various cups, have been attested to alicorn/unicorn horns from the time.[47] One new source of this rare ivory had arrived in European markets—from Norse traders. In the selling of this ivory, a skills premium (in capturing the fabled beast) was exacted from wealthy (horse-owning), aristocratic Europeans, bewildered by the magical properties of such ivory. Because the Norse were renowned sailors, traders, and whalers, of course, the "unicorn" they were capturing, alongside the walrus, was in fact the narwhal. The horned narwhal is found across the Arctic Sea, especially in the deeper seas that hug the coasts of Newfoundland, Greenland, and Baffin Island—each areas of Norse colonization and visitation.

For the Vikings, hunting the narwhal was easy because its buoyancy allowed for easy recovery once killed. Its unique horn, a canine tooth, is an ivory like that of an elephant. When the Vikings traded this narwhal ivory in Europe, they found a devout Christian population awaiting them, eager to believe in the mythical beast. The value of the uniquely spiraled horn was also worth paying for at an inflated price. Because these Europeans had little comprehension of the horned whale at the time, the unicorn exploded into Scandinavian, Scottish, and later British heraldry. The creature can be found in tapestries, such as the splendid *La Dame à la licorne* (The Lady and the Unicorn) on display at Paris's Musée de Cluny, and in drinking horns, cups, and other curiosities that were renowned for their "magical" properties. In Denmark, the royal throne is said to have been made from the mythical creature, albeit later confirmed to be narwhal ivory.[48] The Vikings may have even traded for the ivory from local inhabitants. By around the eleventh century CE, the Vikings would have come into contact with the so-called Dorset culture, a culture also known to have hunted the narwhal.[49]

While the unicorn's origins began as an ox from the Hebrew *re'em*, our modern notion of the flying horned horse may owe some of its origins to the North Atlantic Viking trade, from a time long before Columbus. We tend to think of pillage and destruction when thinking of the Vikings, not shrewd traders cutting off the horns of a whale, selling them as unicorn horns at astronomical prices—all the time keeping quiet about their true origin.

A Genoan Intrigue

Tales of Viking exploration and their trading empire recently began to hold firmer ground. In a 2021 paper presented in the peer-reviewed journal *Terrae Incognitae* by Professor Paolo Chiesa of the Department of Literary Studies, Philology, and Linguistics at the State University of Milan,[50] Chiesa argued that the writings of a fourteenth-century Milanese Dominican friar, Galvaneus (Galvano) de la Fiamma (1283–c. 1345), demonstrated knowledge of a land west of Greenland across the Atlantic. Galvaneus wrote 152 years before Columbus, in his largely unfinished work, the *Cronica Universalis*, of a *"terra que dicitur Marckalada,"* or "a land which is called Markland," situated due west of Greenland. The land being referenced here is recognizable as the Markland (land of forests) referred to by Icelandic sources and identified as being located off the Atlantic coast of North America, perhaps the forests of Newfoundland and Labrador. Galvaneus's reference was probably derived from oral sources heard in Genoa and the broader area and could indeed be one of the first mentions of the American continent in the Mediterranean region. Further to this, the *Cronica* provides some evidence of the extent of knowledge of lands that lay beyond Greenland.

Galvaneus described the area in loose terms; however, although he was writing from a purely oral tradition, the detail is impressive enough for us in the modern era to establish the area he describes:

> Our authorities say that under the equator there are very high mountains, where there are temperate settlements, made possible by winds, or by the shadow of the mountains, or by the remarkable thickness of the walls, or by underground caves in valleys. At the equator there are also many islands that are truly temperate because of the rivers, or the marshes, or the winds, or for reasons that are unknown to us.
>
> And for a similar reason there are settlements beneath or around the Arctic pole, despite the very intense cold. These settlements are so temperate that people cannot die there:

this fact is well known for Ireland. The reasons why this happens are unknown to us. Marco Polo speaks explicitly about this, when he says that there is a certain desert 40 days across where nothing grows, neither wheat nor wine, but the people live by hunting birds and animals, and they ride deers.

Further northwards there is the Ocean, a sea with many islands where a great quantity of peregrine falcons and gyrfalcons live. These islands are located so far north that the Polar Star remains behind you, toward the south. Sailors who frequent the seas of Denmark and Norway say that northwards, beyond Norway, there is Iceland; further ahead there is an island named Grolandia, where the Polar Star remains behind you, toward the south. The governor of this island is a bishop. In this land, there is neither wheat nor wine nor fruit; people live on milk, meat, and fish. They dwell in subterranean houses and do not venture to speak loudly or to make any noise, for fear that wild animals hear and devour them. There live huge white bears, which swim in the sea and bring shipwrecked sailors to the shore. There live white falcons capable of great flights, which are sent to the emperor of Katai. Further westwards there is another land, named Marckalada, where giants live; in this land, there are buildings with such huge slabs of stone that nobody could build with them, except huge giants. There are also green trees, animals and a great quantity of birds. However, no sailor was ever able to know anything for sure about this land or about its features.

From all these facts it is clear that there are settlements at the Arctic pole.[51]

The source of this knowledge is presumably the oral tradition derived from Leif Eriksson, Erik the Red, and other Scandinavian mariners who had explored and settled in Iceland, Greenland, and the North Atlantic throughout the tenth and eleventh centuries.

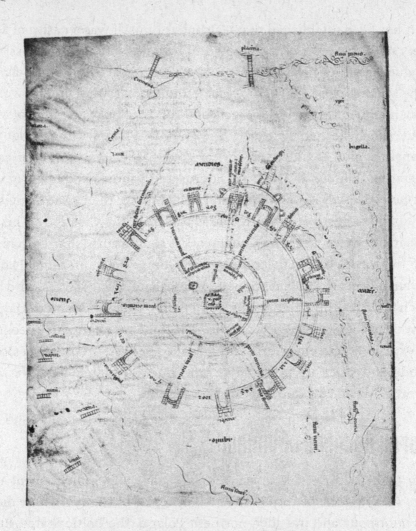

Galvaneus de la Fiamma's Map of Milan

In his paper, Paolo Chiesa extrapolates, using a range of circumstantial evidence, that the origin of this oral tradition can be traced to the then-maritime power of Genoa, which in the fourteenth century (the time *Cronica* was produced) was a major hub of maritime commerce, with territory spanning the Mediterranean and Black Sea. Balaklava in the Crimea, for example, was founded by the Genoese in this era, who named it "Bella Clava," or "beautiful port."

It has been established that Galvaneus himself was a native of Milan, a very much inland city, not known to be a hive of maritime gossip and intrigue, albeit its closest port is Genoa. Further to this, he was chaplain to the Milanese lord Giovanni Visconti and wrote several literary works in Latin, mainly on historical subjects and contemporary accounts of Milan, about which he had firsthand knowledge. When writing about non-Milanese topics, or indeed historical accounts, he was noted for explicitly stating the sources (such as Isidorus and Solinus) and range of views that he had used. His final and unfinished tome, the *Cronica*, envisaged including the history of the whole world from the Creation to his own time, in fifteen books.[52] The actual work is significantly shorter than that, with the abrupt halt in the middle of the fourth book, presumably due to Galvaneus's death. The mention of "Marckalada" occurs in the third book, which includes the Third Age of Humankind, from Abraham to David. In addition to the chronological account, the third book contains a geographical explanation of where areas such as the Far East, Arctic lands, Oceanic islands, and Africa are, presumably capturing the excitement of the recent travels of Marco Polo and Odoric of Pordenone.

Church Records of Vinland

Prior to 1070, an ecclesiastical scholar, Adam of Bremen, spent many years studying the history of the archbishopric of Hamburg. The diocese was enormous and included northern Poland, the Baltic States, Russia, Finland, Prussia, the Scandinavian countries, and all the islands in the north Atlantic except Britain and Ireland. King Sven of Denmark told him "of yet another island discovered in that ocean, which is called Wineland because grapes grow wild there, producing the best of wine. Moreover, that self-sown grain abounds there we have ascertained not from fabulous conjecture, but from the reliable report of the Danes."[53] Indeed, according to some reports, King Olaf II of Norway is said to have visited Vinland in 1016 CE.[54] According to Helge Ingstad, the Icelandic annals for c. 1112 and also in c. 1121 mention that Bishop Erik Gnupsson also set out for Vinland,[55] but Father Ivor Baardson writing in the fourteenth century reports that

Gnupsson never returned. Trade continued between Norway, Greenland, and Vinland, and the settlement that grew around Leif Eriksson's original home became known as Norumbega.[56] This area may have been the country annexed by King Haakon Haakonson in a treaty dated 1262. The annexed territory included Iceland, Greenland, and a place called Landa-nu, which was allegedly discovered by a man called Rolf from Iceland in 1258. Bishop Gissur Einarsson noted that the sailing directions to this land from Iceland were to the southwest, which would bring one to either Newfoundland or Nova Scotia. Thus, despite the fact that this land had been settled before, the term *new* may just have been a stratagem for the king to claim ownership. Documentary evidence supporting the claim to sovereignty by the King of Norway over the "new lands to the west" was plentiful by the mid-fourteenth century. In that century's final decade, Queen Margarette of Norway charged her principal advisor and senior earl, Earl Henry St. Clair of Orkney, with the responsibility of both exploring these lands and exploiting them so that Norway could free itself from the stranglehold on its trade exerted by the Hanseatic League. Before we examine those voyages in detail, let us examine what evidence has accrued for transpacific contact with the Americas.

CHAPTER 6

Transpacific Contact

The swiftest horse can't overtake a word once spoken.
—*Chinese proverb*

A major bulwark in the defense of the "no contact with the Americas before 1492" paradigm is the bold statement that there was no dissemination of flora and fauna from the Americas to the Old World across the oceans prior to that date and, furthermore, that there was no dissemination of Old World plant or animal forms to the Americas until Columbus's famous voyage. Significant progress in consigning that idea to the waste bin of academic history has been made by two American researchers, John L. Sorenson and Carl L. Johannessen. They have found a massive amount of evidence for the interchange of plants, animals, and pathogens from Asia to the Americas and also in the reverse direction. Among their opening statements is this clear and unequivocal one:

> Examination of an extensive literature has revealed conclusive evidence that nearly one hundred species of plants, a majority of them cultivars, were present in both the Eastern and Western Hemispheres prior to Columbus' first voyage to the Americas.

The evidence comes from archaeology, historical and linguistic sources, ancient art, and conventional botanical studies. Additionally, 21 species of micro-predators and six other species of fauna were shared by the Old and New Worlds.[1]

This wide distribution would have been impossible if it were simply due to natural transfer mechanisms, or as a result of early human migrations to the New World via the Bering Strait route. More than half the plant transfers they studied were of flora of American origin that spread to Eurasia or Oceania, at some surprisingly early dates.

The only viable and credible explanation for these phenomena is "a considerable number of transoceanic voyages in both directions across both major oceans that were completed between the

It should be noted that von Wuthenau, writing in 1970, came from a school of now-outdated (and frankly offensive) racial grouping, common throughout his own education. We have retained this quote to demonstrate exploration, not to cause offense.

7th millennium BCE and the European age of discovery."[2] Sorenson and Johannessen were confident that the vessels and nautical skill for the long-distance voyages necessary had been developed by the times indicated. These voyages put a new complexion on the extensive Old World/New World cultural parallels that have long been the subject of bitter debate and controversy. Sorenson and Johannessen's data clearly demonstrate that fauna and flora were extensively shared between the Old and New Worlds across both the Atlantic and Pacific Oceans long before 1492. These shared organisms crossed the oceans via intentional voyages that took place during the eight millennia or more preceding Columbus's first transatlantic voyage. Until recently, suggestions of such early transoceanic voyages have been met with one of two arguments: outright denial on the one hand or by a reasonable demand from critics for "hard" or "scientific" evidence for the voyages, such as a demonstration that numbers of plants were present on both sides of the oceans before Columbus's day.

The parasitic hookworm *Ancylostoma duodenale*, for example, is most prevalent in East and Southeast Asia, and that area is the obvious source from which the organism reached the Americas. *A. duodenale* was at first assumed to have been introduced by slaves brought from Africa. Early in the twentieth century, Fonseca discovered the parasite in an isolated Amerindian population in the Amazon Basin. How did it get there? Early in the lifecycle of this worm, it must inhabit warm, moist soil, and at a later stage, it penetrates a human host's body and settles in the digestive tract. Immigrants who came across the Siberian land bridge would have arrived hookworm-free because the cold conditions would have killed the parasite in the soil. Gerszten Allison and his team established this parasite's pre-Columbian presence in the Americas in 1973 when they found traces of the parasite in a Peruvian mummy dated to about 900 CE.[3] Evidence from other mummies and human coprolites has confirmed the initial find many times over. Then in 1988, Brazilian scientists identified this parasite in remains that were radiocarbon-dated to nearly 7,200 years ago. Given the remoteness of the burial site, the organism's arrival on the coast must have been centuries earlier.

The questions that arise from these findings are: Do they establish conclusively that early human voyagers crossed the ocean to the Americas? Is there some other explanation for the presence of the worm in the New World due to natural forces, independent of human beings? Sorenson and Johannessen state unequivocally, "Absolutely not!" And try as we might, we can think of no alternative and viable explanation either. As early as 1920, the microbiologist Samuel Darling wrote that the hookworm had infested South American tropical forest peoples since before Columbus arrived, and he went on to claim that, if a date could be proven for the parasite in the Americas before European discovery, the only explanation for the parasite in the New World would have to be that it arrived some time before Columbus, in the digestive tracts of infected mariners.

Modern microbiologists assure us that Darling's assessment was correct. In 1982, Ferreira, Araújo, and Confalonieri stated, "Transpacific migrants from Asia by sea *must be* one component of the ancient American population."[4] As early as 1970, Fonseca asserted, "Shared species of parasite

. . . *make it inescapable* that voyagers reached South America directly from Oceania or Southeast Asia." Ferreira and colleagues agreed in 1988: "We *must suppose* that the human hosts for the parasite *arrived by sea.*"[5] Araújo confirmed all these ideas in 1988, when he stated, *"The evidence points only to maritime contacts."*[6]

These facts are vital. Since *A. duodenale* could only have arrived in the Americas living in the bodies of Asians who came by sea, it must be assumed that elements of their culture and their genes arrived with them. Therefore, both cultural and genetic proof by DNA testing will ultimately be found as vessels capable of crossing the Pacific were in use by the sixth millennium BCE.

In biology, a given species arises only once in the course of evolution because each new species develops within a unique set of environmental parameters that is found in only a single geographical location. The plant geographer Nicholas Polunin stated this very clearly: "The chances that two isolated populations will evolve in exactly the same way are incalculably low."[7] When the same species is found to have occurred in the Americas as well as in Oceania, Asia, Europe, or Africa, this demands a rational explanation. However, few seeds are equipped to survive long while floating or move great distances via wind; the odds against successful natural transport of plants are enormous. Thus, anyone who claims a passive, natural mode of transport is obliged to demonstrate precisely how it happened in each individual case. Equally, the idea that humans transported plants across the ocean also requires empirical proof.

In the mid-twentieth century, such cultural proofs were found and caused an academic furor. When the Smithsonian archaeologist Betty Meggers found Japanese ceramics at an Ecuadorian site, she dated the pottery to the third millennium BCE. Thus, Japanese ships had sailed across the Pacific and established a colony in South America. As this was contrary to the prevailing doctrine of "Columbus was the first," Dr. Meggers was promptly denounced by her colleagues, despite the fact that her evidence, methodology, and conclusions were beyond reproach. Her controversial assertion of a prehistoric relationship between the peoples of northwestern South America and of Japan was based on similarities of pottery fragments found in Japan and Ecuador. She contended that Japanese Middle Jōmon pottery was similar to ceramics from the Valdivia site in Ecuador—both dating to between 2000 and 3000 BCE. And, in almost prophetic support of the hypothesis floated by Sorenson and Johannessen, Meggers also stated that plants, pathogens, and parasites of Japanese origin are found among Andean populations.[8]

The formative period in Ecuadorean pottery in the coastal areas has been carbon-dated to 2500 BCE.[9] The earliest phase of this culture is associated with the type of pottery called Valdivian, which is so startlingly similar to pottery used at the same period in south Japan with the Jōmon culture that it is held to be proof of transpacific contact. "Nevertheless the similarities between the two pottery complexes are so striking and the dates so fitly in agreement that a transpacific introduction of pottery at about 2500 BCE seems to be the only explanation of the facts."[10] Thus, the presence of this pottery points to a direct interaction between East and West at a much earlier point in the course of their cultural development than had previously been supposed, and also suggests a rational explanation for the many other parallels in their civilizations. As an odd coincidence, Wallace-Murphy came across the following comment some years ago that may or may not have a bearing on the Eggers discovery when he read a work of the author James Bailey; Bailey claims, "When the Europeans first reached the coast of North West America they found the Indians using Japanese as slaves."[11] Other similar cultural links abound; for example, the ancient ceramics of India are full of interesting parallels with those produced in Meso-America, and anyone familiar with Mexican pieces also feels "at home" with pieces from Siam.[12]

While the cultural connections joining South America with Japan are startling but nonetheless convincing, those linking China and the Americas are almost too numerous to mention. Pierre Honoré claims the Chinese reached the coast of Peru between 500 and 400 BCE. And that people of the Dogon culture of Tongking and Annam extended this contact to Chile and Argentina in the fourth century BCE.[13] There is also a record of a Chinese traveler visiting America across the Pacific in the first millennium CE.[14] Alexander von Wuthenau reports:

> Fifteen years ago, when I began an intensified study of Pre-Columbian terra-cotta heads, I had no intention of making a study of the artistic representation of various races simply because I did not suspect that this aspect existed. On the contrary, what I was looking for were typical "Indian" heads. It was not long, however, before I discovered that in the early, lower, levels, these genuine Indians were not to be found. The earliest figures were those with Mongoloid characteristics and also real Chinese and very Japanese wrestlers, Tartars, all kinds of white people, especially Semitic types with and without beards, and a surprising number of [those with African elements].[15]

On the other side of the Pacific, official Chinese chronicles record that in 219 BCE a fleet under the command of Tzu Fu sailed to the Americas—the land of Fu Sang—with 3,000 young men and women, all young, intelligent, and skilled. And the fleet never returned. The Shih Chi chronicle, first century BCE edition, states, "Tzu Fu found some calm and fertile plain with a broad forest and rich marshes where he made himself king."[16]

It is perhaps not so surprising that in the region of Monte Albán or Izapa, archaeologists have identified the emergence of a totally new artistic style dating to somewhere between 300 and 100 BCE. It has been called the "Itzapan style," characterized by an abundance of intricate scrollwork that archaeologists Robert von Heine-Geldern and Gordon Ekholm identified as being "Chinese." Further research has revealed an incredible level of Chinese Taoist symbolism in this region, along with Chinese Kanji writing, Chinese ceramic toys, Chinese pottery, Chinese jade coins, and the carved faces of Chinese sailors. DNA tests have also revealed a high concentration of Chinese genetic input among the population. All taken into account, this seems to give a clear indication of a significant Chinese migration into this region.[17] This migration also brought with it supplies of steel-tipped arrows and powerful composite bows, which may well have given the Mayan hosts of the new immigrants a distinct advantage in their battles with the Olmecs. Thus, Chinese influence may have exerted a distinct and powerful effect on the rise of Mayan civilization.

Barbara Pickersgill, a botanist who specializes in the evolution and domestication of crops, found no records of plants growing in Mexico that originated in China but did find the opposite: plants indigenous to Central America had crossed the ocean long before the European voyages of discovery.[18] Sweet potatoes, tomatoes, and papayas were found on Easter Island; sweet potatoes in Hawaii; and maize in China and the Philippines. While the maize may have come from South or North America, the other plants must have originated from Mexico, Guatemala, or Nicaragua.[19]

Other, far more complex, cultural links can be found. The process of lacquering is the same in Mexico as it is in China. The decorative techniques used in both countries are so remarkably similar that it is almost impossible for experts to differentiate between them. Theoretically, if somewhat implausibly, this highly elaborate, detailed, and time-consuming process could have evolved simultaneously in both China and Mexico, countries thousands of miles apart, but lacquering is not the only incongruity when it comes to the artwork of western Mexico and China. Both countries have extraordinarily similar and unusual methods of obtaining the dyes they used. Madder red, indigo blue, scarlet, and shellfish purple are obscure dyestuffs producing brilliant colors but requiring complex procedures to extract and fix them. Again, we would argue that these identical processes did not arise independently of each other.[20]

> [I]n many areas where the step of applying these substances as colorants might have occurred, it didn't, and sophisticated application of them . . . is so involved that it seems remarkable that it developed at all, not to say multiple times . . . thus when we find several of these dye-stuffs . . . shared by distant regions, we must consider the possibility of historical contact, and rather intimate and repeated contact at that—especially

in the light of a host of other shared and often arbitrary traits.[21]
... It is inconceivable that these dying processes could have
been accidental, independent discoveries; "a common source
of the two civilizations must therefore be assumed."[22]

In 1970, the *Times* newspaper in London reported that two Leningrad specialists in Oriental antiquity claim that Asian geographers knew of the existence of the Americas in at least 1500 BCE. Lev Gumilev and Bronislav Kuznetsov based their hypothesis on the deciphering of ancient maps of the world in old Tibetan books. The arrangement of countries and continents on the maps conforms to the knowledge of the world by the ancient Sumerians and Chaldeans, the earliest geographers. The Soviet specialists concluded that the data contained in the map was known in Asia in the second millennium BCE: "The honour of the discovery of the Americas probably belongs to ancient Asian travellers." The specialists continued by stating that the ancient Tibetan maps were known to Orientalists beforehand but had been believed to be charts of imaginary lands of fantasy or mystical Buddhist fables. That view changed after a laborious analysis. The two scholars believe that the deciphering of the maps opens the way for interpreting many ancient Indian and Tibetan geographic texts that have so far been regarded as mysterious.[23]

There seems to be a powerful mass of evidence that the Chinese had not merely traded with the Americas but set up colonies from California to Peru (indeed, recent DNA analysis shows conclusively that local peoples in Mexico, Panama, Colombia, Venezuela, and Peru share Chinese DNA).[24] Pre-Columbian Chinese bronze figures were found in Peru, and Nazca figurines of the sun god have a Chinese symbol for heaven on their base. The museum at Teotihuacan has Chinese medallions and Chinese jade necklace decorations that were found at Chiapa de Corzo in the modern state of Chiapas. Don Ramon Mena, one-time director of the National Museum of Mexico, described one medallion as "centuries old . . . carried to America when the Chinese came to this continent."[25] It came as a surprise to us to discover that there were more than a thousand books providing overwhelming evidence of pre-Columbian Chinese voyages to the Americas and that this literature has even been summarized in a two-volume bibliography.[26]

The theory of pre-Columbian contact across the South Pacific Ocean between South America and Polynesia has received support overall through various lines of evidence other than the areas that we have already established. It is known the Polynesians did not necessarily draw maps for posterity; instead, they sang songs that routed their journeys across the vast Pacific Ocean and the islands that they later inhabited. Furthermore, similarities have been noted by the names of edible roots in Maori and Ecuadorian languages (*kumari*) and Melanesian and Chilean (*gaddu*). A 2007 paper published in the Proceedings of the National Academy of Sciences has also put forward DNA and archaeological evidence that domesticated chickens had been introduced into South America via Polynesia by late pre-Columbian times.[27] Perhaps we should be looking eastward for evidence of the "first Columbus."

CHAPTER 7

Maritime Trade in Europe I: The Mediterranean

*Perhaps I am afraid of losing Venice all at once,
if I speak of it, or perhaps, speaking of other
cities, I have already lost it, little by little.*

—Marco Polo

The reasons that lay behind European exploration of the North Atlantic and the Americas in the mid- to late-fourteenth century arose from the trading patterns affecting three countries that developed between the eleventh and the early fourteenth centuries. Those countries are the city-state of Venice and the kingdoms of both Norway and Scotland. After gaining the throne at the Battle of Bannockburn, Robert the Bruce, the King of the Scots, established viable trading links with France, Denmark, the Low Countries, Scandinavia, and the Baltic seaports. The trading patterns that emerged in Northern Europe over the next century were increasingly dominated by a consortium of German seaports that became known as the Hanseatic League, or the Hansa, that used the Teutonic Knights as their mercenary army. The first recorded meeting of the maritime towns, also known as the Wendish group, consisting of representatives of the cities of Lubeck, Hamburg, Luneburg, Wismar, Rostock, and Stralsund, took place in 1256 CE. From that day forward, they began to use their concerted power with growing efficiency to gain a monopoly on trade within Northern Europe and the Baltic.[1] The rise of the Hansa occurred at a time when the greatest trading nation in the European world was passing through a period of decline due to developments further east.

Venice had dominated trade in the eastern Mediterranean for centuries,[2] controlled the trade routes to the Holy Land, virtually monopolized trade with Byzantium, and completely controlled both the spice and silk trades. The Aegean was, in effect, a vast Venetian lake, and Venice maintained her dominance over Mediterranean commerce in the teeth of stiff competition from her major rivals, the city-states of both Genoa and Pisa. The Venetians were always on the lookout for ways and means to extend and strengthen their trading empire and, by 1314, the year of Bannockburn, had established trading links with Western Europe as far north as Flanders and England. However, further expansion northward was severely restricted by the growing power of the Hanseatic League.

The Foundation of La Serenissima

The strange thing is that the immensely powerful city-state of Venice was founded by a very frightened people who created the city in a lagoon to protect it from successive waves of invaders.[3] It is built on marshland and an area of 22 square miles of water shallow enough for men to wade through that is intersected with deep-water channels that can carry the merchant shipping that sustained its economy for centuries. The various invaders, Alaric the Goth and Attila the Hun, should be thanked and immortalized for their role in stimulating the creation of Venice—La Serenissima—still one of the most beautiful cities in the world.

Isolated and protected by the lagoon, the city achieved a remarkable degree of self-determination during the later years of the Roman Empire. By the mid 500s, it possessed the most powerful fleet in the Adriatic. In 726 when the Byzantine Empire was in crisis, the pope in Rome encouraged all the Byzantine provinces on the Italian peninsula to rebel against their political masters in Constantinople. It was then that the lagoon communities chose one of their leaders, Ursus of Heraclea, to be their duke, or dux. Similar developments occurred elsewhere, but the emerging city-state of Venice was, and remained, different in that the position of its duke, or doge in local dialect, was an elected one and not hereditary. In the early years the doge was elected by the mass of the people, but that soon changed into an election by the members of the Grand Council alone. There were 117 people elected as doge until Napoleon dissolved the Venetian Republic at the end of the eighteenth century.[4]

In 1095, at the start of the First Crusade when Pisa and Genoa, both trading rivals of Venice, sensing new opportunities in the East, began to prepare their fleets, Venice hung back. The shrewd merchants of Venice knew that war was bad for trade, and they were reluctant to get involved in religious hysteria. Furthermore, the goodwill of the Arab merchants and Seljuk Turks was absolutely essential if the caravan routes to Asia, the main means of supply for both silks and spices, were to be kept open to them.[5] Furthermore, Egypt was the major clearinghouse for the spice trade from India and the East and also provided a ready market for European timber and metal. Thus, it was not until after 1099 and the fall of Jerusalem that a Venetian fleet of twenty-two sails made its way to the Holy Land.[6] This provoked a battle with the Pisan fleet near the coast of Rhodes. Venice was the winner, capturing twenty Pisan ships and over 4,000 prisoners. As shrewd businessmen, the Venetians had put their own commercial interests before those of the Crusades, defeating the Pisans before striking a blow for the Christian cause. The fleet docked in Jaffa in the middle of June 1100. Godfroi de Bouillon, the Protector of the Holy Sepulchre, went to Jaffa to negotiate with the Venetians but, owing to ill health, had to return to Jerusalem, and his cousin Count Warner de Gray took his place.

The terms the Venetians demanded reflected their commercial interests, not their piety. In return for help and support of the new Crusader state, they demanded free trading rights throughout the land, a church and a market in every Christian town, a third of any town or city they might help to capture, and the entire city of Tripoli, for which they would pay an annual tribute.[7] The speed with which the Crusader state accepted all the Venetian demands reflected its desperate need of maritime support. The first city to be subjected to a joint attack was Haifa, which surrendered on July 25, one week after the death of Godfroi de Bouillon. The citizens of Haifa were treated in the same merciful, Christian, and loving way that the inhabitants of Jerusalem had been in 1099: all of them—Christian, Jew, or Muslim—were slaughtered without mercy. It is doubtful that the Venetians played any part in this massacre, for this was the standard treatment by the Crusaders for the inhabitants of any captured city. As the Crusading armies consolidated their hold on the Holy Land, the Christian population increased, and opportunities for trade and profit expanded with the population. To gain a dominant role in this emerging market and limit the influence of both Genoa and Pisa, a second Venetian fleet of one hundred sails arrived in October 1110. This fleet rendered significant assistance at the siege of Sidon, and the Venetians were rewarded with a substantial grant in the city of Acre. The massive increase in trade with the Holy Land stimulated Doge Ordelafo in Venice to nationalize the shipbuilding industry in the republic and create a large complex of dockyards, foundries, and workshops that became known as the Arsenale.[8] Over the ensuing decades, the port of Venice became one of the principal centers of activity of their close allies, the Knights Templar, whose leaders had strong family connections with leading members among the Venetian nobility. The famous Templar war galleys were constructed in the shipyards of their Venetian allies.

It is alleged that Pope Urban III died of shock at the news of the fall of Jerusalem to Saladin's army on October 2, 1187 CE.[9] The new pope, Gregory VIII, promptly called another crusade, and for once, Venice responded promptly and enthusiastically because, with the collapse of the Crusader state, trade had declined drastically, and it was economics rather than piety that inspired Venice to act. A war fleet carrying an army from Italy, England, France, Denmark, Germany, the Low Countries, and Sicily set sail from Venice at Easter 1189.[10] Among this multiracial army were some distinguished figures, including King Richard the Lionheart of England and King Philippe Augustus of France. On their arrival in the Holy Land,

Acre was besieged and fell to the invaders after two years. The outstanding contributions of the Venetians to this victory lay mainly in providing the transport and grabbing the spoils.

The Sack of Constantinople

The indication of the Venetians' true sense of piety and obedience to papal diktat came in the early stages of another crusade. After the death of Saladin in 1193 CE, the chance of retaking Jerusalem looked bright and, in 1201 CE, the Venetian Republic agreed to transport 4,500 knights and their mounts, 9,000 squires, and 20,000 infantry, and provision them for nine months. The cost for all of this was estimated to be 84,000 silver marks, and out of a sense of devotion and piety, Venice agreed to provide fifty fully equipped war galleys in exchange for a 50 percent holding in all conquered territories. It is appropriate to note at this time that during the negotiations leading up to this agreement, there was no mention of which city or country was to be the target of this crusade. The ordinary crusaders believed that they were going to the Holy Land; many of their leaders were more focused on Egypt, while the Venetians, who had just concluded a profitable trade agreement with the Sultan of Egypt, had distinctly different ideas.[11] Somewhere there was a leak, and word got about that Egypt was the intended destination. At this, many Crusaders made their own way to the Holy Land, and many more simply returned to their homes. In consequence, less than 30 percent of the expected forces arrived in Venice. As the Venetians had kept their side of the bargain, they understandably demanded payment in full and refused to allow any ship to sail before payment had been received.[12] The end result shamed all concerned. Instead of sailing to liberate the Holy Land from the Saracens, the fleet sailed to the Christian city of Constantinople and plundered it mercilessly. This was the beginning of the end for the already weakened Byzantine Empire. Thus, the greatest treasure house of art, culture, and knowledge in the East was looted and pillaged in a destructive orgy of violence, Christian against Christian. The Machiavellian prime mover in this supreme act of betrayal, the Republic of Venice, filled her communal coffers to overflowing.

Other events again pitted Christian against Christian, once more involving the Venetians, but this time in the Holy Land itself when, in 1256, Genoese forces occupied the monastery of San Sabas at Acre that the Venetians also claimed for themselves. Fighting soon broke out.[13] It spread and rumbled on for nearly five years and involved nearly all the allies of the two principal antagonists. The principal allies of the Venetians were the Knights Templar. The rival military order, the Knights Hospitaller, sided with the Genoese. The matter was finally brought to a faltering conclusion only after a land battle in which the Templars were victorious and the Venetians won a series of naval engagements.[14]

By this time Venetian shipbuilding skills were probably the best in the Western world, and the Arsenale, their shipyards and armaments manufactories, were a hive of constant and highly profitable activity. Technological progress provided even more potential for profit; for example, in Europe, the use of the marine compass appears from the late twelfth century, aiding navigation and assisting the art of mapmaking, which, in turn, led to more accurate charts. The ship's rudder underwent substantial improvement that, in its turn, led to larger ships and allowed maritime trade to continue on a year-round basis for the very first time. And, according to the English historian John Julius Norwich, it was the opening up of trade between Venice and England and Flanders that

> more than any other single factor led to the introduction in about 1320 of a revolutionary new ship design. Until this time oars had never been used for commercial vessels[;] they had been kept for warships, where high speed and manoeuvrability [were] essential . . . Now merchantmen too needed to move quickly—and with more precious cargoes to carry, they demanded increased protection. The answer was found in the merchant galley.[15]

The early merchant galleys were of 150 tons burden, and they were equipped with sails and carried 200 oarsmen, who were not slaves but free men. While the expense of maintaining such a large crew was high, this cost was far outweighed by the larger profits that accrued from faster voyages less vulnerable to piracy. An additional bonus was that the increased maneuverability substantially reduced the risk of shipwreck, and the oarsmen could be armed in the event of attack.

The Venetian Trading Network

The political and economic necessities of wide-ranging trading links transformed the Republic of Venice from a city-state to an almost colonial power in the Mediterranean. It had colonies in Greece and also had satellites and cities dotted throughout the Mediterranean. Some were acquired as the result of campaigns against pirates—those on the Dalmatian coasts, for example. Others were simply glorified trading posts, such as Modone, Acre, and Negropont. On January 24, 1339, Venice signed a peace treaty that gave it territory on the mainland of Italy near Padua and gained, thereby, an assured source of corn and meat.[16] In Padua itself, the house of Carrara was restored to power under the benevolent guidance of the doge. In other towns and cities, Venice installed a watered-down version of the system that worked so well in the Serene Republic itself. Large cities were administered by a *podesta* and small towns by a *capitano* or *provveditore*—positions broadly similar to that of the doge. The manner of their election was somewhat Byzantine, and their independent powers were strictly limited. In Venice itself, the doge—despite all the outward pomp and ceremony—was the servant of the Council of Ten, which was, in effect, the Grand Council's cabinet.[17] In the dependent territories, the podesta was the servant of the rector, who was always a Venetian who owed his responsibilities to the Senate of Venice and the Council of Ten.

By 1340, the presence of a Turkish armada of 230 ships threatened the Eastern Mediterranean and menaced not merely Venice, but all of southeastern Europe. The Turkish lines extended to within 60 miles of Constantinople. The weakened Byzantine Empire was riven by dissent and was virtually bankrupt. The only powers that could possibly stem the Turkish advance were the rival city-states of Venice and Genoa, but the rivalry between them prevented any possible alliance.

Despite the Turkish threat, Venice was at the peak of its prosperity and began to adorn the capital with new buildings, glorious art, and all the outward trappings of power. In January 1341, the reconstruction of the doge's palace began creating the facade known and loved today. Its design is one of stark contrast to the seats of power of mainland cities in Italy—each being a true reflection of the relationship between rulers and ruled. The centers of power in the mainland cities are threatening and forbidding, seemingly designed to protect the rulers from the anger of the people. The doge's palace, on the other hand, is light and airy and appears to celebrate a mutually beneficial union between rulers and ruled. It is an architectural "hymn of praise to God," erected as though as an act of gratitude for the prosperity, beauty, and serenity of the city of Venice. The historian John Julius Norwich describes it as being imbued with "a dazzling fusion of grace, lightness and colour."[18] The artistic and architectural frenzy of rebuilding, however, did not blind the Venetian authorities to the escalating menace posed by the Turks.

The Black Death and Nearly Continuous War

Venetian and Genoese merchant ships had one form of cargo in common—rats infected with the plague bacillus. And in 1348, these unwelcome stowaways brought the Black Death to Europe. By the end of March, the plague was killing over 600 people a day in Venice. When the epidemic eventually subsided, more than fifty families of the nobility and 60 percent of the population of the Republic of Venice had been completely wiped out. The situation in Genoa was about the same. This disaster did nothing to diminish the rivalry between the two states, and a series of wars continued for some years. A war with Hungary that ended in 1358 cost the Venetians all of their Dalmatian colonies. In 1377, Venetian interests were threatened by the Genoese, who, in alliance with the fading Byzantine Empire, attacked Tenedos, which lay at a strategic position near the Hellespont and controlled the entrance to the straits and the Sea of Marmara. If Tenedos fell, Venice would lose all access to Constantinople and the Black Sea. Venice triumphed. Then the war came closer to home in the Venetian lagoon itself.

One Venetian fleet under the command of Pisani defeated the Genoese off the coast of Anzio, but about a year later at Pola, he was soundly defeated and a mere six battered Venetian galleys limped back home to Parenzo. Pisani was imprisoned and barred from holding any office in the Republic for five years. Thus, Venice deprived itself of one leading admiral at a time when another, Carlo Zeno, was far away in the eastern Mediterranean. Zeno's fleet was off the Turkish coast, and all that was left to defend Venice were the battle-scarred galleys at Parenzo. Luckily, the Genoese had lost their admiral as well, and thus, their fleet remained inoperative until a replacement arrived from Genoa.

Chioggia

During the brief respite, the entire population of Venice was mobilized to strengthen its defenses. Many rich families put their entire fortunes at the disposal of the state; nobles fitted out war galleys or subsidized the cost of defensive works. Genoese allies, including an army of 5,000 Hungarians, attacked Venice's mainland territories.[19] Soon an advance squadron of Genoese sails was sighted from the Lido that had been fortified by stout walls and a triple defensive ditch. Three heavy hulks were chained together to block the entrance to the lagoon, and the piles and stakes used to mark the shoals in the channel were stripped from the seabed to confuse the invaders. A Venetian army of over 4,000 horsemen and 2,000 infantry, along with a large body of crossbow men, garrisoned the Lido di Venezia, a chain of small islands, and armed boats prevented communication between the Genoese fleet and its land-based allies. These defenses were marshalled in the nick of time for, on August 6, the Genoese fleet of forty-seven galleys under the command of Pietro Doria hove into sight at Chioggia, the malodorous marshlands at the southern end of the Venetian lagoon.

En route southward towards Chioggia, the Genoese had burned Grando, Caorle, and Palestrina. After capturing Malamocco, they sailed to Chioggia to try and unite forces with its land-based allies. Three thousand men defended Chioggia, but it fell on August 16, 1379, after a spirited defense that cost both sides dearly. Now, for the first time in Venetian history, a fortified town within the lagoon that commanded a deepwater channel that led to the heart of the city was in the hands of the enemy. The people demanded that Admiral Pisani be released from prison, and he was put in command of the city's defenses. A defensive wall across the Lido was completed within fourteen days; a boom was stretched across the western end of the Grand Canal, and this was protected with ships armed with rockets. The Genoese decided to starve the city into submission rather than risk a costly frontal assault, and this gave Pisani the time to make the city virtually impregnable. Then Giovanni Barbarigo destroyed three Genoese ships guarding a mainland fort. As this was happening, Giacomo de Cavalli led a slow but steady advance south along the Lido and recaptured Malamocco. As winter was approaching, the Genoese withdrew into Chioggia. Pisani swooped because Chioggia was almost landlocked, and he blocked all three channels out of it by sinking a large stone-filled hulk in each of them. Venetian forces could effectively close any remaining possible escape routes.[20] The blockading expedition set out on December 21, 1379, led by Pisani and accompanied by the doge. Once the hulks were in place, the Genoese were locked up tight in Chioggia. Whether or not this blockade could have been sustained throughout the winter storms is a moot point, but on January 1, 1380, Carlo Zeno and the main Venetian fleet moved into sight. The blockade of the Genoese in Chioggia continued, and an attempt by another Genoese fleet to relieve them failed. Over 4,000 starving Genoese in Chioggia surrendered unconditionally on June 24. The entire city took to the water to greet the doge, who had remained with the fleet throughout the long blockade. The victory was one for the entire people, with great credit accruing to Pisani, the doge, and the city's timely savior, Carlo Zeno—a member of one of the oldest and most respected families in Venice. Carlo Zeno, known as Il Leone (the Lion) was one of three brothers, Nicolo and Antonio being the other two. All three brothers had important roles to play in extending Venetian trading links and, as a result of contacts made to certain northern capitals in Europe, in transatlantic exploration also.

CHAPTER 8

Maritime Trade in Europe II: The Western Coasts

After we came home, we found ten men red of blood and dead.

—THE KENSINGTON RUNESTONE

The controversial order known as the Knights Templar was founded in mystery; rose to military and economic prominence with remarkable speed; and was suppressed after a sequence of mass arrests, torture, and accusations of heresy. However, this noble order was far more than merely monastic or even military. Its activities transformed the economic life of Europe and laid the foundations for our present capitalist society. Its network of holdings, farms, commanderies, and bases near the main pilgrimage routes of Europe not only gave protection to the pilgrims but also made the roads safe for merchants to travel free from the risk of robbers. The Templars created a banking system that was trusted so that gold or money did not have to be carried by the individual merchants, and this further reduced the financial risks of overland trade. The Templars also had a fleet, transporting troops, armaments, and pilgrims to the Holy Land; they also acted as a most profitable merchant arm of the order. All the order's commercial activities were designed to fulfill one primary purpose: to make a profit that would fund military activities in the Holy Land. The Templars acted like a modern multinational conglomerate, trading in wine, wool, grain, cloth, fish, and a host of other commodities that would turn a profit. They owned land from the Baltic in the north to the Balearic Islands in the south, from Portugal in the west to the Holy Land in the east, and their fleet, with ships built in the Arsenale in Venice, was modern, well equipped, and supremely seaworthy. As they paid no taxes either to kings, emperors, or church hierarchy, they plied their maritime trade for profit wherever it could be made. However, one word of caution must be given at this juncture: despite long-standing legends and traditions that claim the Templars reached the Americas, or the plethora of fantasists who scatter Templar attributions on American historical sites like so much confetti, there is no credible evidence whatsoever that members of this knightly order ever crossed the Atlantic. As both of us are Templar fans and old-fashioned romantics, we believe that they indeed may have done so, but there is no proof, direct or indirect, that they did. So, Templar voyages to America must remain classified as legendary.

The commercial activities of the Knights Templar began to alter the balance of power in medieval Europe. With the rise of the mercantile classes and an economic climate that allowed the accumulation of capital, power began to shift from the landed aristocracy to the newly emerging merchant class. Markets throughout Europe began to grow and prosper. Maritime trade was no longer the principal route for commerce, but it still remained one of the most important, as it was both faster and easier than overland trading.

There was an important trading network off the west coast of Europe that linked the Low Countries, England, Scotland, and Scandinavia that grew and flourished after the tenth century. Trade was vitally important to all of these countries, particularly to Norway, where from the beginning of the thirteenth century, most of the necessities of life had to be imported.[1] Trade to Norway continued along the old Viking routes from Greenland and Vinland, especially the fur trade, but contemporary records demonstrate that Norway was in a state of growing dependence on imported foodstuffs, especially flour, grain, and malt. Domestic production of grain was by now insufficient, owing to the rising population of the Nordland fisheries. Norway was blessed, however, in having valuable goods for trade with the rest of Europe, such as fish, butter, hides, and furs. Dried fish became the principal item of export during the Middle Ages, coupled with the expanding population of the Rhine lands; Southern Germany and the Baltic became the most important market for Norwegian fish after a series of wars of succession that lasted from 1130 until 1240. Norway's earlier fur trade with the Friesians had slowly died down, but new trading links with various parts of Germany, England, and Flanders began to replace it. Through these routes Norway could obtain cloth, salt, and metallic products in exchange for dried fish, butter, meat, walrus teeth, and furs. While more and more merchants began to establish themselves in Bergen, from the eleventh until the mid-thirteenth century, Norway's principal trading partner was at first England, despite the earlier history of Viking raids and occupation. Thus, ships from the north sailed every summer laden with, as mentioned earlier, ivory and furs from Vinland and walrus teeth from the Arctic to Norway; in exchange, the Norwegians received the luxuries of the south.[2] These included goods from French and Flemish markets, such as a variety of cloths, lead, spices, ale, beans, and honey, that were exchanged for timber, furs, whale meat, dried fish, fish oil, and goods Norway had imported from the Black Sea. This trade with England continued throughout the twelfth and early thirteenth centuries, by which time other actors had taken the stage, including the Dutch and the Germans. The role of the German trading cities increased inexorably during the later years of the thirteenth century as a result of their ability to supply Norway with grain. A treaty signed by King Haakon IV and the City of Lubeck laid the foundations for the subsequent German domination of Norwegian trade.

The rising importance of German cities in north European trade arose from the fact that the main route from the Mediterranean to the north was via the Rhine Valley. Furthermore, as the Baltic countries became colonized, German trade increased. This trade was epochal in economic history and led to the formation of the great trading bloc known as the Hanseatic League. In 1320, German merchants of Wisby, the chief city of

Gotland, issued a maritime code that was enforced throughout the Baltic and ultimately became the basis of modern maritime law. However, Wisby's dominance was short-lived, as Lubeck grew in importance. Strategically located on the highway that crosses the narrow strip of land separating the North Sea and the Baltic, it became a dominant factor in a trading network that linked Hamburg, London, Norway, and Novgorod. The derivation of the term *Hanse* has been disputed, but it seems to have designated an armed company or guild. From the start, there was no ambiguity about the emergent Hanseatic League's primary purpose—"to maintain a monopoly of trade by excluding all rivals and to preserve in their own hands the commercial prerogatives they had already acquired in Flanders and England."[3]

The growth in both wealth and importance of the Hanse during the fourteenth century reflected its success in attaining its objectives. Lubeck had gained control of the salt mines in Luneburg that gave the city even greater commercial clout, as the growth of the fisheries along the Scania coast would have been meaningless without the salt to preserve the herrings. Ultimately, the Hanseatic League became a confederation of cities, similar to a state. At its peak it consisted of some seventy to eighty cities. It became a great political and economic power in its own right and, by its monopolistic policies, exerted a stranglehold over the Baltic and northern European trade routes. A variety of factors had led to the Hansa's domination of Norwegian trade: firstly, a series of blockades that led to suffering and starvation among the people; secondly, the parlous financial condition of the royal family in Norway; and thirdly, the growing monopoly by the Hanse. The single-minded aim of the German merchants was to furnish Europe with Norwegian fish while keeping the fishermen in their debt. For Norway and its people, something had to change, and other sources of food supply had to be sought in order to break the Hanse stranglehold that now effectively forbade goods entering Norway except in ships belonging to the Hanse itself.

Events in the Kingdom of Norway seem almost to have been conspiring to turn eyes west across the Atlantic. The colony in Greenland, despite the harsh climatic conditions, had survived for more than 350 years and had established and maintained trading links with Norway, Bristol, Flanders, and Cologne.[4] Early in the 1340s, strife broke out between the colonists and the Inuit; and a priest, Ivor Baardson, led a fleet of volunteers from the eastern to the western settlement to help combat the Inuit.[5] When he arrived, he discovered that the Inuit were in total control and that the settlers had departed as a group. Indeed, according to another report by Bishop Oddson in Iceland, the Greenland settlers had given up the true faith and fled to join the other Viking people in Vinland.[6] Further confirmation of this rapid desertion by some of Greenland's population can be found in the records of *Peter's Pence* sent to Rome by the colonists, which declined appreciably after 1342.[7] These reports reached Norway in 1348. It was some time before King Magnus was able to act; however, in 1354 he wrote a letter authorizing a special expedition to Greenland under the command of Sir Paul Knutson:

> We desire to make known to you that you are to select men who shall go in the Knorr [a royal vessel] . . . from among my bodyguard and also from the retainers of other men who you wish to take on the voyage, and that Paul Knutson the commandant shall have full authority to select such men who he thinks are best qualified to accompany him, whether officers or men.[8]

The purpose of the expedition was to bring the apostates back to Christianity.[9] It is believed that Knutson first sailed to Greenland to learn whatever he could about the colonists who had fled and also to recruit a pilot for the voyage to Vinland. Vinland was renowned for its climate and fertility and was the most plausible destination for the fugitive colonists. To mount an effective search of Vinland demanded that Knutson find a safe harbor with a defensible and fertile place for an encampment to use as a base.[10] According to Hjalmar Holand, Knutson split his party into three: one small group and at least one ship were based in the St. Lawrence estuary or Hudson's Bay; another penetrated deep inland; and the third was based at Norumbega, the supposed site of Leif Eriksson's original settlement.

According to Holand, the fate of one of these parties is inscribed on the Kensington Runestone that was discovered in Minnesota in 1898. Holand cites a date of 1362, and we translate the inscription as

> [We are] 8 Goths [Swedes] and 22 Norwegians on a journey of exploration from Vinland far to the west. We had camp . . . one day's journey north from this stone. We were out fishing one day, after we came home [we] found ten of our men red with blood and dead. AVM [Ave Virgo Maria] save us from evil . . . ten men by the sea look after our ships 14 days journey from this place . . . 1362[11]

Picture of the Kensington Runestone: George T. Flom—Foldout illustration to the book *The Kensington Rune-Stone: An Address*

This translation of the Kensington Runestone and Holand's claim that it is authentic were about as popular as a rattlesnake in a lucky dip among American academic historians. The dispute over the authenticity of the Runestone had been prolonged and very bitter indeed. When first found, it was immediately denounced as a forgery despite being embedded in the root system of a tree. The idea that a forgery had been there long enough to have tree roots wrapped around it was a question that was never addressed. However, over the last twenty years or so, the authenticity of this artifact has been grudgingly accepted by the academic world in the USA.[12] However, it has then been quietly ignored in the hope that the public will remember the controversy and the cries of fraud rather than register its authenticity.

The majority of European historians who have studied Knutson's expedition have come to a consensus that placed Norumbega at or near to present-day Newport, Rhode Island, on the natural harbor of Narragansett Bay.[13] This consensus arises from a combination of several factors: the precision with which this area matches the description in the *Flateyjarbók*; the nature of the superb natural harbor, which would have attracted a seafaring people like the Vikings; and the various stone artifacts found there. Few members of the Knutson expedition managed to return to Europe,[14] but information brought back by the survivors regarding the death of the Bishop of Greenland indicates that they returned to Norway around 1364. Jacob Cnoyen, a Belgian at the court of King Magnus, confirmed this and recorded those eight survivors reached Norway in 1364.[15]

While the Knutson expedition was still in progress, an important exploration of the North Atlantic took place; it was led by an English monk, Nicholas of Lynne. He explored the west coast of Greenland and Hudson's Bay, and he was known as "the man with the Astrolabe." He was able to estimate latitude with this new instrument, and it is recorded that Nicholas gave one to Ivor Baardson.[16] The voyages of the man with the Astrolabe were recorded in the book *Inventio Fortunatae*, copies of which were given to the King of Norway and to Pope Urban V.[17] According to

American historian Gunnar Thompson, *Inventio Fortunatae* translates as the "Discovery of the Fortunates," and he then defines "the Fortunates" as the legendary isles that the Romans found in the far west beyond the Atlantic. Norway soon found a leader to both explore and seek further profit from the Atlantic—Earl Henry St. Clair of Orkney.

Baron of Roslin and Earl of Orkney

Commit thy work to God.

—Motto of Clan Sinclair

The long and colorful history of one man in Scotland stands out as truly exceptional—Earl Henry St. Clair of Orkney—deemed "Worthy of Immortal Memory." How did a Scottish lord become the leading nobleman of Norway and cross the Atlantic Ocean twice? To explain that, we have to examine the history of the St. Clair Lords of Roslin—the Lordly Line of the High St. Clairs. Any examination, however cursory, of the history of this line demonstrates the courage and commitment of this noble family. The first baron of Roslin, William "the Seemly" St. Clair, was granted the lands for his dutiful service in protecting Princess Margarette on her journey to Scotland to marry the king. Sir William was killed protecting his adopted land from an English invasion.[1] His son, Henri de St. Clair, served along with other Scottish knights in the First Crusade[2] and was present at the capture of Jerusalem.[3] Over the centuries the St. Clairs defended the border against countless English invasions and also took part in the inner councils of the Knights Templar. Yet another William St. Clair destroyed three English armies on the same day in 1303, before returning to Roslin Castle to consummate his marriage. A memorial in Roslin village commemorates this tripartite victory. The same William and his son Henri are believed to have led the Templar charge at the Battle of Bannockburn in 1314. The grave marker of Sir William with its Templar symbolism now rests in Rosslyn Chapel.[4] (The names *Roslin* and *Rosslyn* are interchangeable. Both names are corruptions of the Scottish Gaelic *Riasg Linne,* which means "peat moor near a waterfall.")

Henri's son, yet another Sir William St. Clair, set out with his brother John and Sir James Douglas to carry the heart of King Robert the Bruce to the Holy Land. En route they heard that the Spanish king was fighting the Moors, and they volunteered their services to aid the king. At the Battle of Teba on August 25, 1330, they were cut off by the Moors and heavily outnumbered. They threw the casket containing Bruce's heart into the midst of the enemy and charged after it and were killed. The Moors were so impressed with their bravery that they returned the bodies of the Christian knights and the casket to their Spanish opponents.[5] The bodies of all three knights and the casket containing Bruce's heart were returned to Scotland. Due to the death of the St. Clair heroes of Teba, the barony passed to another William de St. Clair,[6] who married Isabel, the daughter of Malise Spera, Earl of Stratherne, Caithness, and Orkney.[7] Isabel gave birth to a son, Henry St. Clair, in the Robin Hood Tower of Roslin Castle in 1345.[8]

Drama pervaded the life of Henry St. Clair from the very start, as the plague reached Scotland in 1348 when Henry was an infant. This disaster killed far more Scots than the English ever did, and it has been estimated that over one-third of the population perished. According to family histories, the survival of the St. Clairs in general—and Henry in particular—is consequent on them having been bathed in the healing waters of the "Balm Well" a few miles from Roslin Castle. Indeed, it is recorded that on a daily basis they smeared their bodies with the oily waters of the well. This is not quite so unlikely an explanation as it first appears, for the oil content was, in fact, a form of insecticide that might well have prevented any bacillus-laden flea from biting the body beneath. Henry succeeded to the family title and lands after his father's death in battle in Lithuania. Many Scottish nobles were engaged in that campaign, trying to raise funds to pay a ransom demand of 100,000 marks for King David II of Scotland, who had been captured by the English. Thus, Henry became "Baron of Roslin, Baron of Pentland Moor in free forestry, Baron of Cousland, Baron of Cardain Saintclair and a great protector and keen defender of the Prince of Scotland." Quite heavy responsibilities for a thirteen-year-old boy. A later historian, Lord Henry Sinclair, writing in 1590 informs us that Henry was also a knight of the French order of St. Michael.[9] In 1363, five years after he succeeded to the Barony of Roslin, Henry was appointed ambassador to Denmark and took up residence in Copenhagen for the next two years. One of his first official duties was to attend the wedding of ten-year-old Princess Margarette of Denmark to King Haakon VI of Norway. Attending this ceremony began a friendship between Henry and Margarette that lasted until his death.

It was in 1364 that Henry first came into contact with Carlo Zeno, who was touring the capitals of Northern Europe in company with Philip de Mézières, the chancellor of King Peter of Cyprus, to promote a new crusade.[10] This crusade resulted in a large fleet of over 300 ships sailing to Egypt and indulging in the traditional outpouring of Christian love in Alexandria, where the population were put to the sword. After this rather brutal episode, Henry was nicknamed "Henry the Holy" by one of his brothers. Returning from the crusade, Henry married his childhood sweetheart, Janet Halyburton. Henry's mother never let him forget that, through her, he was the rightful heir to the Earldoms of Orkney, Caithness, and Stratherne.[11] The succession to the earldom of the islands had been in dispute since the previous earl, Erngisle, had been deposed for his part in a plot against King Magnus II of Sweden.[12] The three grandsons of the late Earl Malise Spera, namely Henry St. Clair, Alexander de Arde, and Malise Spera, were all legitimate contenders for the earldom. Orkney historian J. Storer Clouston claims that the true heir was most probably Alexander de Arde, but Henry's claim was based on Earl Malise's will, which left the title to Henry's mother and her heirs.[13] To reinforce his claim, Henry could also cite his direct lineal descent from Earl Rognvald the Mighty.

To Henry's dismay, one of his rivals, Alexander de Arde, was appointed as Governor of Orkney and a commissioner for the king on June 30, 1375, but no appointment was made to the earldom. Alexander used his time to build up relations with leading members of the island community during his one-year tenure of office. Orkney was in dire need of strong leadership, as it had descended into near anarchy with the local bishop constantly at loggerheads with the king's representatives. The behavior of this aberrant bishop was such that two commissioners sent by the archbishop to investigate the situation reported:

> He [the bishop] had appointed "aliens, vagabonds and apostates" for a short period of time for a commission which he put into his own pocket. As to his method of spending these ill-gotten gains, he occupied himself so frequently with hawking and clamorous hunting and that kind of levity—to say nothing of other things—that he attended little or not at all to the government of the church.[14]

As a result of the bishop's depredations and greed, his misappropriations reached such a level that it was virtually impossible for the king's bailiff, Haakon Jonsson, to collect rents and taxes for the king.[15] This failure added considerably to the financial pressures upon the Kingdom of Norway at a time when its trade was under the malevolent control of the Hanse. To add to its burdens, Norway now had to contend with the Hanse importing furs from Russia in direct competition with its own trade originating in Greenland, Markland, and Vinland. The straw that threatened to break the camel's back was an influx of pirates, who began to harry the shipping on which both the islands and the Kingdom of Norway depended. Henry seemed the ideal strongman who could be expected to restore peace and order to the islands, boost revenues, limit the financial depredations of the bishop, and put an end to the piracy. Furthermore, he had one other vital qualification: he could pay the sum of 1,000 English gold nobles sterling (around £230,000 in 2022) for the title. Time may reveal if Henry's appointment was merely a matter of money. Or was it the result of his close relationship with the Norwegian crown? Or had the aspiring earl another string to his bow, an agreement with the Zenos of Venice that might solve Norway's problems once and for all?

Henry St. Clair was formally installed and invested with the earldom of Orkney on August 2, 1379. In the installation document, his rivals, Malise Spera and Alexander de Arde, were instructed to cease their claims and demit their rights so that the king of Norway would suffer no further vexation from them. Orcadian historian J. Storer Clouston lists the remaining important terms of the installation document as follows:

1. On three months warning the Earl shall serve the King, out with the Orkneys, with 100 men or more, fully armed.

2. If Orkney or the land of Shetland is invaded, the Earl shall defend it, not only with the aid of the islemen, but with the whole strength of our kin, friends and servants.

3. The Earl shall not build castles or other fortifications in the islands without the King's consent.

4. He shall cherish and protect the lands and inhabitants of Orkney, cleric and lay, rich and poor.

5. He shall not sell or wadset any lands of the earldom.

6. He undertakes to assist and provide for the King or his men if they come to the isles.

7. He promises not to raise war, litigation or dissention that might cause damage to Norway.

8. If he commits notable injustice to anybody he shall answer to the King.

9. He shall attend the King whenever summoned.

10. He shall not violate any truce or peace made with other countries by the King.

11. He shall not make league with the Bishop of Orkney, nor to enter into or establish any friendship with him unless with the good pleasure and consent of our said lord, the King, but that we assist him against the said bishop until he shall do what of eight or deservedly, he ought to do in those

things which our said lord the King desires or may reasonably demand of the said bishop.

12. The Earl's] heirs are to seek inflefment in the earldom from
the King.

13. The earl to pay 1000 gold nobles sterling to the King.[16]

The importance of the earldom of Orkney in Norwegian terms can
hardly be exaggerated. Not only did the isles of Orkney and Shetland produce badly needed revenues for the king, but also the strategic importance arising from their geographical position was truly enormous. They
were the gateway and the gatekeepers to the Atlantic and the colonies of
Iceland, Greenland, Vinland, and Markland. As a base to combat the piracy
that was now endemic in the North Sea, they were ideal. Most importantly,
they could be used to establish new trading links with the Venetians via
the west coast of Ireland that might, at long last, break the stranglehold
exerted by the Hanseatic League on trade between the Mediterranean,
England, Flanders, and Norway. However, the islands had to be defended,
not only against the pirates but also against control by the Hanse.

The earldom of Orkney was the sole surviving earldom in the Kingdom
of Norway, and the earl, or *jarl*, was the senior nobleman in the kingdom taking precedence over the rest of the aristocracy.[17] In consequence
of this, the earl's signature on official documents came after that of the
Archbishop of Nidaros and before those of the bishops and other nobility. He was viewed as akin to royalty and entitled to use the honorific
"Prince."[18] His power in Orkney was almost absolute and carried with it
the right to issue coinage, make laws, and remit crimes. When issuing new
laws, he wore a crown, as he was regarded as being second only to the king
himself.[19] Henry arranged a dynastic marriage for his children: his heir,
another Henry, married Egidia Douglas, the granddaughter of King Robert
II of Scotland. His second son, John, was married to Ingeborg, the daughter
of King Waldemar of Denmark.[20]

Henry was installed as Earl of Orkney by King Haakon VI of Norway at
Marstrand, near Tønsberg, Norway, the year before the king died in 1380.

Haakon's widow, Queen Margarette, became Regent, as their son Olaf was too young to rule in his own right. This may well have had a bearing on why Henry was granted permission to build a castle at Kirkwall, which was in seeming breach of one of the terms of his installation. Thus, in accordance with the military principle of Clausewitz—"first secure your base"—Henry created a strong base for himself and his troops. This castle, like many other St. Clair castles, had a sea gate and thereby could be supplied by water. The castle, which is now long gone, was described in the following terms:

> I protest to God that the house has never been beget without the consent of the Devil, for it is one of the strongest holds in Britain—without fellow.[21]

Henry also gave a solemn pledge to the Crown:

> I do promise to the most excellent prince and my lord, the Lord Haakon, King of Norway and Sweden the illustrious, that I shall in no way alienate or pledge or deliver as security the land or islands of the country of Orkney away from my lord the aforesaid king, his heirs and successors, or surrender them without the consent of my lord the above-mentioned king, his heirs or his successors.[22]

This document was sworn in front of important witnesses, including the Bishops of St. Andrews and Glasgow; Earl William Douglas; George, Earl of March; and a plethora of barons and knights. A second document was a contract generated and signed by King Robert of Scotland, who formally denied that Scotland had any claim to the earldom of Orkney and recognized King Haakon's right to give the said earldom "to our beloved relative Henry Earl of Orkney." Without such clarification, Henry would have been in an ambiguous and potentially invidious position because, as Baron of Roslin, he owed his allegiance to his lord and sovereign, the King of the Scots. In his position of Earl of Orkney and the premier earl of Norway, however, he owed allegiance to King Haakon of Norway and his heirs. Royal approval of Henry's action in building the castle was evidence that Henry and his heirs held the earldom for three generations and, using the castle as his base, he was able to commence the complex and difficult task of bringing order to the chaotic situation in both Orkney and Shetland.

CHAPTER 10

The Earl Consolidates His Power

*There are some places where history just grabs
you by the jugular. This is one of them.*

—Simon Schama

Henry had a considerable advantage when he took over as earl because of his family connections. The Norwegian bailiff in 1364 was his uncle, Thomas St. Clair, and the families of Berstane, Clouston, Craigie, Cromarty, Peterson, Petrie, Heddle, Halero, Ireland, Kirkness, Linflater, Ness, Paplay, Rendall, Scart, Scalter, and Yenstay, all leading families in Orkney, are, according to the genealogist Nicolas Cram-Sinclair, all recognized as septs and dependents of the Clan Sinclair. Eric Linklater, a writer with an international reputation, noted that "Unlike his immediate predecessors, Earl Henry I Sinclair identified himself with Orkney and apparently lived there in considerable style."[1] Henry's grant of the earldom was, in effect, a royal license to gain power by good governance, force of arms, diplomacy, family connections, and guile. The situation was, in reality, both anarchic and chaotic; his opponents were many and varied and included all lawbreakers, pirates and smugglers, illegal tax collectors, and, above all, the corrupt and venal bishop. His earlier rivals for the earldom, Malise Spera and Alexander de Arde, were forbidden to leave Norway and thereby nullified as a threat for the moment. Henry's new castle gave him a fortified base to counter the bishop's palace that housed a large garrison that the bishop used to enforce his illegal theft of lands, taxes, and rents.[2] By opposing the predatory bishop, Henry was not only doing his duty to the king but was also making himself popular with the people of Orkney. Indeed, in 1362, there was a popular revolt against the prelate, and the records show that "then was heard the mournful tidings that Bishop William was slain in the Orkneys . . . killed or burnt by his flock."[3] The Chapter of St. Magnus in Kirkwall asked the pope to nominate John, the parish priest, at Fetlar to be the new bishop, but at that time there were two popes, and it was some time before a new bishop was appointed and installed. Earl Henry used that time to consolidate his position and restore the lands and property that had been illegally seized to their rightful owners or to the king or the earldom.

The Earl's Growing Sea Power

When Henry first acceded to the earldom, Orkney and Shetland each had a population of about 25,000 people. They exported fish, pork, sheep, and hides to Scotland and to the Hanseatic League. They imported timber, flax, salt, pitch, wax, and pewter ware. The potential tax revenues were high if they could be collected. Getting to grips with the situation, Henry became more and more aware of the stranglehold on this trade exerted by the Hanse. Under Henry's firm rule, the islands entered what was probably the most prosperous era in their history. As he gained increasing political and military control over Orkney itself, he began to realize that he urgently needed a fleet to extend his mastery over the outlying islands and over Shetland. Orkney is relatively treeless, so Henry sent back to Roslin for timber from the Pentland forests that had good pine and oak trees. He used this timber to build a battle fleet of thirteen ships: two galleys, one long-decked battleship, and ten decked barks.[4] Frederick Pohl claims that Henry armed this fleet with cannon when he learned of their use at Chioggia.[5] This is doubtful due to the lack of contemporary records claiming such use.

The only notable exception to this was that of the Morosini Chronicle, which records that

> One 13 July 1380 . . . The Genoese who were enclosed in Chioggia . . . from every corner were trying to damage our galleys with their cannon. . . We had 33 galleys altogether with their crews ready at their oars for rowing and to do what was necessary. [They were] equipped with cannon and with cannon balls in great quantity.
>
> On August 10 they [Venetian galleys of the relief force] reached Rodo and took on water . . . and 12, enemy galleys were near, that is in the harbour of Vieste [in Apulia] and being advised of our arrival . . . they fled at once. Our fleet pursued them courageously, and some of our galleys drew near and some were killed and others wounded by cannon and crossbows from one side to the other.[6]

Again, even with this in mind, it still remains doubtful that cannons would have been transported to the earl in any fashion.

(left) Coat of Arms of Henry I Sinclair; (middle) Coat of Arms of Earl William Sinclair; (right) One quarter of Henry Sinclair's Coat of Arms

The importance of sea power to the earldom of Orkney is shown in Henry's coat of arms. In the second and third quarters, we see the Engrailed Cross of the St. Clairs in argent (silver) on a sable (tincture of black) background. The first and fourth quarters display an armed galley in gold against an azure background within a double tressure counter-flowered in gold.[7] This heraldic crest combined the blazon of the Lordly Line of the High St. Clairs with naval power as the double tressure, indicating virtually royal rank.

Although Earl of Orkney, Henry also was still Baron of Roslin and had responsibilities to discharge there. He visited Roslin on June 8, 1384, to invest his cousin, James St. Clair, Baron of Longformacus, with some land, although he would be back there again to repel an English army under King Richard II when, in 1385, he marched into Scotland. Henry spent several weeks campaigning against the invaders and eventually carried the war into England, laying siege and pillaging the area around Carlisle, a usual response to English expeditions into Scotland. In all, the earl spent several months on this campaign before returning to Orkney to begin preparations for the subjugation of the Shetlands. On one visit south, in 1387, he signed an agreement in Edinburgh with Malise Spera and then had to go to Scandinavia later that same year.

Queen Margarette was Queen Regent until her son, Olaf, died unexpectedly at age sixteen in 1389. Henry, as one of the main electors for the throne of the three kingdoms, had to attend court. It was on February 2, 1388, that his good friend Queen Margarette was elected for life as Queen of Norway and Sweden and recognized as the rightful heir and regent of Denmark. She had wisdom beyond her years and was known as "the Semiramis of the north."[8] This shrewd and intelligent lady knew that her subjects would have preferred a king to rule over them, and to preserve future continuity and stability for her kingdom, she adopted the five-year-old Eric of Pomerania as her heir. The queen persuaded the Council of Electors to recognize Eric as the rightful heir to the crowns of the three kingdoms, and she was left with the power as regent until he came of age.[9] The charter confirming Eric's rights of succession was signed by Vinold Archbishop of Trondheim; Henry St. Clair, Earl of Orkney; a variety of bishops; and the nobles of the Council of Electors.[10] When Eric was proclaimed as King of Sweden at Helsingborg, Henry was there and he also attended Eric's coronation as King of Norway in 1389. The day that Eric was proclaimed as the King of Sweden, Henry signed a solemn and binding agreement with Haakon Jonsson, the Royal Bailiff of Norway, stating:

> Let it be known by those present that we, Henry St Clair, earl of Orkney and Baron of Roslin, with our heirs, are held and bound To a man of nobility, Haquin the son of John or his successors, in 140 pounds sterling of Scottish gold, to be paid to him or his heirs or sure deputies at the Church of St Magnus the Martyr in Tingwell in Shetland, at terms in the year, without fraud or trick; that is the first term being St Lawrence's day 1390, 40 pounds, at the second term the same day of 1391, 40 pounds, at the third term the same day of 1392, 40 pounds and at the fourth term the same day 20 pounds, all at the same place. If we or our heirs fail to pay Haquin Johanson or his successors, they may seize all our rents for their loss and the delays with escheats from the islands of Sanday and Ronaldsay in Orkney, not lessening in any way the sum of 140 pounds, and they will enjoy the rents and escheats till fully paid. . . . Our seal is appended at Helsingborg Palace.[11]

By this agreement, Henry had bound himself to pay four substantial sums of money to the King's bailiff on an island on which he had not yet set foot and, if he failed to do so, would lose a large slice of the revenues of Orkney that he had subdued. Behind the complex conditions, we can see that Earl Henry has now established himself as the crown's powerful representative in Orkney, and he was now being commanded to extend his rule to the Shetlands for, unless he could bring those under the rule of law, he would not be capable of making the due payments under this agreement. Earlier he had been bound to make similar payments in Kirkwall to the king's bailiff, and now he was deemed to have established his power base there, he was ready to bring the Shetlands under his control. Indeed, it is clear from the date of signature and the first due date of payment that the Queen was aware that Henry now had sufficient troops and ships to wrest control over the Shetland Isles.

In the spring of 1390, Earl Henry was at Scone in Scotland to pay homage to King Robert III, who had just acceded to the Scottish throne. It was only after Henry had discharged his duties in that respect that he was in a position to try to extend his rule to the Shetland Isles. This was far from an easy task because the Shetland population was over 25,000, all of vigorous Viking stock who might well resist him; furthermore, there could be no element of surprise, as his intentions were well known. His first objective was the island of Fer (Fair), about halfway between Orkney and Shetland. This small isle, which is only about 3.5 miles long by half a mile wide, has a very rugged coast surrounded by rocks and reefs that are scoured by strong tidal currents. Indeed, there were only three possible landing places for his fleet. No one has recorded the details of his landing there, but negotiations with the islanders began immediately. As negotiations continued, the islanders snatched up their weapons and ran toward the coast, where a large vessel had been driven onto the rocks.[12] Like the Cornish people, the Fer islanders plundered all wrecks and tended to slaughter the crews of any vessel that foundered on its shore. The crew were clinging desperately to the wreckage and made no attempt to reach the shore because the murderous intentions of the islanders were all too obvious. Henry dispersed the islanders with his troops and had his men cast lines onto the wrecked vessel. The vessel's crew were foreigners, but Henry communicated with them in the one language that every educated man in Europe knew—Latin. The ship was Venetian, and the captain was Nicolo Zeno, the brother of Carlo Zeno, the hero of Chioggia. Henry had met Carlo both on the crusades and also when the Venetian visited the Norwegian court in 1364.

Venetian ships made annual voyages to Flanders and England but were restricted in any attempt to venture further north owing to the monopoly exerted by the Hanse. Venetian trade had suffered a decline as increasing Turkish dominance in the Eastern Mediterranean had restricted their activities there, and the Hanse monopoly in the north prevented any expansion of activity in that direction. Carlo Zeno, as a result of his visit to the Norwegian court, was well aware of both the dangerous situation of Norwegian trade and the potential for profit if he could only establish viable trading links with the principal provider of fur and fish from across the Atlantic. When at the Norwegian court, he had heard reports of the Knutson expedition and also knew of the exploration of the north Atlantic by Nicholas of Lynne, so he was well aware of the realities of north Atlantic trade. In the light of the Hanse's ban on foreign shipping in Scandinavian waters, why did the Venetians risk the wrath of the German monopolists by sending one of their vessels this far north in such an act of provocation? Is there a plausible explanation?

Indeed, there is. We have mentioned Venice's pressing need for an expansion of trade as well as Norway's similar predicament. Carlo had met Earl Henry and knew that he was under pressure to make effective and beneficial change to the trading patterns of Orkney. Furthermore, after the Crusade against the Cathars and the prosecution and suppression of the Knights Templar, under the repressive rule of Holy Mother the Church, who was safe in Europe? If the most powerful defenders of Christendom, the Templars, had been butchered and suppressed, was anybody safe? There was, therefore, a clear and pressing need not only for new trading opportunities but also for lands to settle that lay beyond the reach of the dreaded Inquisition. A new commonwealth was needed wherein men of talent could trade and prosper without fear. Now was the opportunity that we suspect had been long planned for: Henry, in cooperation with the Zenos, could employ his fleet, using the islands as stepping stones across the Atlantic, and found settlements that would be clearly based on freedom of trade and freedom of belief.

Nicolo Zeno was truly Carlo's brother. Skilled in navigation, he had been the captain of a galley in the war against Genoa. One of the richest men in all Venice, he had also been Venetian Ambassador to Ferrara. On his travels, he constantly kept his family informed of his movements, thoughts, and plans by a constant stream of letters, a practice continued by his brother Antonio. A later descendant edited and published these letters as the "Zeno Narrative." In one such letter, Nicolo describes sailing past the straits of Gibraltar, sailing northward toward England, passing Flanders, and then on north again. He describes the storm that wrecked his aforementioned vessel, and he names the site of his wreck as Frislandia, a corruption of the Latin version of Fer Island. He also describes "a great lord who ruled certain islands called Portlanda which lay to the south of Frislandia."[13] Portlanda is now accepted as an Italianate variant of an older name for Orkney, namely Pentland.[14] As well as being described as the lord of these isles, Henry is also named as the duke of certain estates in Scotland. Both Nicolo and the men under his command were invited to serve in Henry's fleet, where their seamanship and navigational skills were employed to great effect. Within a relatively short space of time, Henry's courage, diplomacy, and skill—reinforced by his army and his fleet—resulted in the subjugation of the Shetlands to the rule of Norwegian law. With that accomplished, Henry thanked captain Nicolo for "the preservation of his fleet and the winning of so many places without any trouble to himself."[15]

In grateful recognition and gratitude for all Nicolo had done in his service, Henry dubbed him a knight.[16] The other Venetians were rewarded with very handsome presents. The island had grown rich from the trade in fish: ling, herring, cusk, and cod, which were in great demand in Scotland, England, Flanders, Brittany, and, of course, Norway and Denmark. The people of Shetland made prolonged north Atlantic voyages, and the island also was often host to many hundreds of fishing vessels from Western Europe. Money was little used; they worked on a barter system, often paying their taxes in butter, fish oil, and homespun cloth. The Zeno Narrative recounts that Sir Nicolo asked his brother Antonio to commission a ship and come and join him for further exploration. The Narrative continues:

> Since Antonio had as great a desire as his brother to see the world and its various nations and to make himself a great name, he bought a ship and directed its course that way. After a long voyage full of many dangers, he joined Sir Nicolo in safety and was well received by him with great gladness as his brother, not only by blood but also in courage.[17]

Henry Controls His Earldom

Henry made his main base in the principal port of Shetland and instituted a series of beacons so that he could signal from one island to another all the way back to Kirkwall in Orkney.[18] As Henry now had full control over the Shetlands, the king's bailiff could now land without hindrance, and Henry's representative made the payment due under the terms of the agreement. Henry left Sir Nicolo in command while he returned to Scotland, via Kirkwall, to attend the coronation of King Robert III. Henry's possession of the Shetlands is confirmed in a charter he signed on April 23, 1391, that confirmed his donation of lands in Aberdeenshire in return for his half-brother's renunciation of any rights in the earldom of Orkney and Shetland:

> To all who shall see or hear these present, Henry St Clair, Earl of Orkney and Lord of Roslin, safety in the Lord! I concede to my brother, David St Clair, because of his claim through our mother Isabella Spera in Orkney and Shetland, all the lands of Newburgh and Auchdale in Aberdeenshire, to return to if his heirs fail.[19]

Less than three months after this document was signed, the seething rivalry between Henry and Malise Spera came to a bloody and final end. It all erupted at the annual Lawting held at Tingwall in Shetland. This annual legislative and judicial assembly was held on an island in a small lake that was accessed by a stone causeway. In 1391 a case involving Malise Spera was brought to judgment. Despite the terms affecting him in Henry's installation document and a treaty of amity with him, Spera had unlawfully retained lands that were not his. He arrived accompanied by a body of armed men, in total contradiction to law and custom, and attempted to resist judgment. A contemporary account records that

> it seems that the Earl was about to hold a court to settle the legal rights of the parties concerned. A conflict taking

place, the dispute was terminated by a strong hand . . . Malise Spera with seven others was slain in Hjatland by the Earl of Orkney.[20]

Shortly after this brief but brutal conclusion, Earl Henry fought and won a conclusive victory against the pirates. By now his actions had gained both Henry and Nicolo Zeno a well-deserved reputation for skill, effective action, and courage.

By early 1392, the Kingdom of Norway had, as a result of its battles with pirates and the Hanse, almost completely lost its power at sea. As a stopgap remedy, while shipbuilding could take place, Queen Margarette commenced correspondence with King Richard II of England to gain permission for Earl Henry to travel to London with the intent of leasing three warships for the Norwegian fleet. Safe conduct was granted on March 10 to "Henry Seint Cler, Comes Orchadie et Dominus de Roslyne" to enter England with a party of no more than twenty-four people. Any fugitive from English justice was excluded from the safe conduct, and the document itself expired on September 29 the same year.[21] It is highly probable that Henry brought some of his Venetian advisors with him for the visit. Further to the leasing of vessels, the London journey was also to purchase rigging, tools, and naval armaments. All in all, the stage was now set for further exploration to the west.

CHAPTER 11

The Zeno Exploration of the North Atlantic

*Joyfully to the breeze royal Odysseus spread his
sail, and with his rudder skillfully he steered.*

—HOMER

There is some dispute over exactly where Henry established his fort in Shetland. According to Frederick Pohl, it "was in all probability at the water's edge in Lerwick."[1] Someone my co-author Wallace-Murphy trusted who has made a prolonged and in-depth study of the St. Clair voyage, Niven Sinclair, has a different opinion that sounds far more plausible. The Zeno Narrative states that Henry built his fort in Bres, which most modern scholars assume to be Bressay. Niven Sinclair claims that the foundations of this castle are still visible on Learaness, a place that in Henry's time would have been on the tip of a long peninsula, the tip of which is now an island. This spot gives a superb view of the approaches to Bressay Sound that comprises both the north and south harbors of Lerwick.[2] Sir Nicolo Zeno remained here and, in 1393, prepared three small barks for an exploratory voyage. He first sailed north in the month of July and landed in Egroneland, or Greenland.

Here he found a monastery of the Order of the Preaching Friars and a church dedicated to St Thomas by a hill which vomited fire like Vesuvius or Etna. There is a spring of hot water there that is used to heat both the church of the monastery and the chambers of the Friars. The water comes up into the kitchen so boiling hot that they use no other fire to cook their food. They also put their bread into brass pots without any water, and it is baked as if it were in a hot oven.[3]

There is a site in Greenland that mirrors this description accurately, and it lies just north of the main eastern settlement. As cited in Pohl, archaeologists such as Alwin Pederson, Helge Larsen, and Lauge Koch reported the existence of formerly active volcanoes and thermal springs on the east coast of Greenland.[4] Dr. William Herbert Hobbs, the geologist, identified some ruins nearby as those of St. Olaf's monastery, one that had been described several centuries earlier by Ivor Baardson, who wrote that the hot springs there "were good for bathing and as a cure for many diseases." Dr. Hobbs reports that in respect of the descriptions in the Zeno Narrative, evidence for all of these have been found there. One nineteenth-century historian, Dr. Luka Jelic, tells of an account written by papal emissaries in 1329 who reported to Pope John XXII that there were two monasteries in Grotlandia (Greenland): one called Gardesi (Gardar) and the other called Pharensi—a name suggesting a Pharos, or lighthouse, indicating its proximity to a volcano. The Zeno Narrative goes on to describe how the hot springs were used to irrigate the gardens before flowing into the harbor. Despite the nine-month long winter, the harbor never froze because of the thermal springs draining into it. The warmth of the water ensured that fish and seafowl were there in abundance to feed the monks. However, ships that reached the harbor immediately before winter were trapped nonetheless because the seas immediately beyond it froze, and these vessels had to wait for the thaw before being able to leave.[5] The winter in that part of Greenland was so severe that Sir Nicolo became ill, and he returned to Fer Island, where he died. His brother Antonio inherited all his wealth and honor and succeeded him as Earl Henry's admiral. An account of

Nicolo Zeno's voyages of exploration and his death was reported by Marco Barbaro in *Discendenze Patrizie* in 1536, some twenty-two years before the eventual publication of the Zeno Narrative.

Another exploratory voyage was soon being planned based on a local story of interesting provenance. An Orkney fisherman recounted that some twenty-four years previously, four fishing boats had been driven westward by a severe storm and landed on a place they called Estotilanda, over 1,000 miles from Iceland. One boat was wrecked, and its six-man crew were brought to a nearby city, where the king found an interpreter who spoke Latin and asked the men to remain with him. The fisherman described this land as "very rich and abundant in all things." The inhabitants were "intelligent and as well-versed in the arts as we are and that they had obviously had dealings at some time with our people for in the King's library were Latin books which they did not now understand."[6] These people traded with Greenland, exporting furs, sulfur, and pitch; grew corn; and made beer. They did not have the compass, and because of this, the fishermen were held in great esteem. They were sent on a voyage to the south to a place called Drogio. On their arrival, locals captured them, and one fisherman who taught these locals to fish with nets was spared; the others were all killed and eaten. The surviving fisherman lived among them for thirteen years, moving among them and teaching them all the art of net fishing.[7]

Henry's informant described this country as "a new world" peopled by locals who were uncultivated, had no metal, and who lived by hunting with wooden spears. They were very fierce, fighting among themselves, and their chieftains and laws differed from tribe to tribe. Eventually, a ship arrived that took this informant home, where he met with Earl Henry.

No one will ever be certain whether this traveler's tale was the trigger point that provoked Henry into action, whether it was merely one issue among many others, or if it was merely a clever piece of camouflage used to disguise the long-planned nature of the enterprise. Henry was already well aware of the New World across the Atlantic from the Viking sagas and from the reports of the Knutson expedition. He also knew of the exploratory voyages of Nicholas of Lynne, as well as the long-standing trading links between Greenland, Markland, and Vinland. It is also reasonable to speculate that Henry had already disclosed much of this information to Carlo Zeno and his brothers. However, it would have been most imprudent to disclose any of this information in letters home that might ultimately have been intercepted and disclosed to either the Inquisition or the dreaded Hanse.[8] The first notice of the intended voyage is to be found in a letter written by Antonio Zeno that states:

> [T]his nobleman is now determined to send me out with a fleet towards these parts. There are so many that want to join on this expedition on account of the novelty and the strangeness of the thing, that I think we shall be very well equipped, without any public expense at all.[9]

The eventual editor of the Zeno Narrative, a later Nicolo Zeno, added after the preceding passage that Antonio "set sail with many vessels and men, but that he was not the commander as he had expected to be." Earl Henry himself was going to be the leader, and in this manner, the expedition went ahead.

Earlier authors, in their attempts to estimate the size of Henry's fleet for this voyage, have been somewhat too imaginative in their assessments of both the size of the fleet and the number of men Henry took with him. Fantasy has had free rein in previous descriptions, which have alleged that Earl Henry took with him the Knights Templar, Cistercian monks, or that he carried vast treasure, or in one patently ridiculous account, transported the Holy Grail across the Atlantic. There is not one shred of credible evidence to support any of these crazy allegations. The Knights Templar had been suppressed some seventy-five years before Henry sailed. Was it even reasonable to suppose that he would have taken a number of monks with him on what was both a trading and exploratory voyage? We think not!

Henry's original fleet of two galleys, one battleship, and ten barks had been augmented by the addition of the Venetian galley brought by Antonio Zeno. When we take into account Henry's duty to protect Orkney and Shetland while he was away, it is virtually certain that he left at least one galley, the battleship, and six or seven barks behind for defensive purposes.

The remaining ships were one Venetian galley and its 200 oarsmen, one Orkney galley, and three or four barks for scouting purposes. Such a fleet would have been more than capable of making the planned voyage and of defending itself against any piratical attack that might occur.

Earl Henry and his fleet sailed west from Orkney and Shetland, island hopping in the traditional Viking manner to cross the Atlantic. We read, in the Zeno Narrative, that

> Then at last we discovered land. As the seas ran high and we did not know what country it was, we were afraid at first to approach it. But by God's blessing, the wind lulled and then a great calm came on. Some of the crew then pulled ashore and soon returned with the joyful news that they had found an excellent country with a still better harbour. So, we brought our barks and our boats into land, and we entered an excellent harbour, and we saw in the distance a great mountain that poured out smoke.[10]

An investigation in force by one hundred armed men was sent toward the smoking mountain with instructions to return with accounts of any inhabitants that they might meet. The main body remained with the ships, took on stores of wood and water, and caught a large quantity of fish and seafowl that were abundant there.[11] The Narrative continued:

> While we were at anchor here, the month of June came in, and the air in the island was mild and pleasant beyond description. Yet as we saw nobody, we began to suspect that this pleasant place was uninhabited. We gave the name of Trin to the harbour and the headland which stretched out onto the sea, we called Capo di Trin.[12]

The historian Frederick Pohl made a brave attempt to use this passage to date the voyage and the landfall. He assumed, not unreasonably, that the naming of this place was made because they made landfall on Trinity

Sunday. Trinity Sunday is, however, a moveable feast, and Pohl quoted the possible dates as being June 6, 1395; May 28, 1396; June 17, 1397; and June 2, 1398, and opted for the last date. If one reads the Zeno Narrative with care and diligence, we find that Henry and his party arrived at this place *before* the beginning of June. The passage in question actually reads as follows: "While we were at anchor here, the month of June came in"[13]—thus, the expedition had anchored before the end of May. If Pohl was correct in his assumption that the naming of the harbor and headland celebrated the expedition's landfall on Trinity Sunday, then the inevitable conclusion must be that the date of this moveable feast was May 28, 1396.

The key passage in any reasonable attempt to identify the actual point of landfall is the description of the smoking mountain and the information brought back by the party sent to investigate it:

> After eight days the hundred soldiers returned and told us that they had been through the island and up to the mountain. The smoke came naturally from great fire in the bottom of the hill, and there was a spring giving out certain matter like pitch which ran into the sea, and there were great multitudes of people, half wild and living in caves. They were very small in stature and very timid; for as soon as they saw our people, they fled into their holes. Our men also reported that there was a large river nearby and a very good and safe harbour.[14]

Because Greenland is treeless and the landfall was well wooded, it is reasonable to assume that this area was Markland, which had traditionally been a source of timber. Furthermore, the information brought back by the scouting party indicates that this place is either an island or a peninsula. We can estimate the distance to the smoking mountain as being about three days' travel—allowing for the time necessary to investigate the mountain itself and the harbor. Thus, the smoking mountain must be within a 45- to 60-mile radius of the original landfall. No island off the east coast of North America is large enough to take three days to cross, so Henry and his men had landed somewhere on the mainland itself. All the known deposits of pitch in the east of the Americas can be found in Trinidad, the upper reaches of the Orinoco River, and in Alabama, Kentucky, Missouri, and Texas. None of these areas lie within 1,000 miles of the northeast coast where Henry might have landed. The puzzle was solved by Dr. William Herbert Hobbs, a geologist from the University of Michigan, who named the one site that fits the Narrative's description as near the present-day town of Stellarton in the Pictou region of Nova Scotia. There one can often find a fire near the base of a hill in close proximity to a river of pitch-like substance that runs into the sea. A stream known as Cole Brook flows into the estuary of the East River that empties into Pictou Harbour. Below Pictou, this river is tidal and, at low tide, the muddy bottom is black with oily waste. The local Native American people, the Mi'kmaq, speak of an opening near the riverbank that has burned and smoked many times over the centuries. This is caused by coal seams underground that catch fire: one such fire that started in 1870 burned for twenty-six years. When my co-author Wallace-Murphy visited this area, he was shown around by Leo F. McKay, a retired civil servant, who informed him that coal mining had been stopped in this part of the world for safety reasons. Too much methane in the coal seams and too many explosive mining disasters and the consequent loss of life set a price that was far too high to pay. However, Wallace-Murphy was in total agreement with Frederick Pohl in identifying the site of the smoking mountain with Stellarton.

Identifying the Landfall

The landfall, Trin Harbor, must be within a 60-mile radius of the smoking mountain at Stellarton. From the Narrative we learn that as the party approached land, the wind was from the stern and was blowing from the southwest when they sailed toward the headland. Furthermore, beyond that headland was a superb harbor. This description matches up exactly with Chedabucto Bay on the northeast coast of Nova Scotia. The southern extremity of this bay is a headland that juts into the sea as described in the Zeno Narrative. Today that headland, named Cape Canso, is the one that Henry and his party christened Cape Trin. Furthermore, at the eastern end of Chedabucto Bay, which at first glance is a continuous and well-wooded stretch of coastline, there is a small opening that is masked by a sand bar, and it leads into a stretch of sheltered water that runs inland for over 10 miles, Guysborough Harbor, which was Earl Henry's safe haven at the end of his first transatlantic voyage. Frederick Pohl first made the case for this landing over fifty years ago,[15] and not only did Wallace-Murphy accept it without reservation, but so do many others who have followed him. To commemorate this landfall, the Clan Sinclair Association erected a memorial in the form of the upturned prow of a Viking ship, which rests in a public park near the waterside. On the southern shore of the bay lies another, far more permanent memorial: a large rough-hewn granite standing stone that bears a plaque installed by the Prince Henry Sinclair Association of North America, stating that this spot is the most likely site of Henry's first anchorage.

The area surrounding the harbor has not changed all that much. It is still well wooded and the perfect habitat for bear, moose, and other game. When Henry and his party landed in the final years of the fourteenth century, it was the perfect hunting ground for the Mi'kmaq people, who are the Native Americans of this region. The Zeno Narrative described them as "timid," an insulting term that belies the truth; we would perhaps use "circumspect" or "cautious" as being the more likely description of their attitude when they saw a large body of men dressed in a manner that was literally outlandish: "Who were these people, and what can we discern about their attitude, culture, and beliefs?"

CHAPTER 12

A People of Peace

Remember to walk a mile in his moccasins.

And remember the lessons of humanity
taught to you by your elders.

—MARY T. LATHRAP

The Mi'kmaq nation, who are part of the Algonquin or Wabanaki Confederacy, have lived in the area of Henry's landfall; they have inhabited the lands now known as the Maritimes or Maritime provinces for over 10,000 years—in fact, since the end of the Ice Age.[1] The Maritime provinces include New Brunswick; Nova Scotia, which includes Cape Breton Island; and Prince Edward Island, and are northeast of New England in the United States. Other tribes and nations of the Algonquin Confederacy reach as far south as Cape Hatteras in North Carolina. This strong confederation of tribes was a defensive alliance, giving protection against the warlike Iroquois, and it lasted until the beginning of the eighteenth century, when a combination of disease and wars with the English made it ineffectual.

The Mi'kmaq people lived in seven districts, each of which was autonomous, having its own defined territory that was administered by a council of elders and a district chief. The council of elders was composed of village chiefs and other senior members of the community. Each district had the power to settle disputes; allot hunting and fishing rights to designated families; and, in the final analysis, make war or peace. The seven districts were Kespukwitk, Sipekne'katik, Eskikewa'kik, Unama'kik, Epekwitk Aqq Pitkuk, Siknikt, and Kespek.[2] Villages varied in size from 50 up to 500 inhabitants in each. While it is impossible to count them at the time of Henry's arrival in 1396, an estimate of the total population in that era is about 100,000. The district of Eskikewa'kik, the land of the "skin dressers," comprised most of the northeast coast of Nova Scotia and includes Chedabucto Bay and Guysborough Harbor, while Epekwitk Aqq Pitkuk, "the explosive place," spans the town of Stellarton, Pictou Harbour, and the smoking mountain. The Grand Council made up of the seven district chiefs chose one from among them to be the Grand Chief, who ruled the entire nation. These were the trusted servants of their people, for their real powers were those allotted to them by the various districts. Decision-making was by means of persuasion, example, and consensus rather than by decree in the European manner. As the real basis of power and influence lay with the district councils that were open to all who wished to attend, the statement that the Mi'kmaq people had developed "one of the most democratic political systems that has ever existed" may well be a simple statement of truth.[3] The name *Mi'kmaq* has an interesting derivation that tells us a great deal about the people it describes. It is said to arise from their friendly and kindly way of greeting fellow tribesmen, friends, allies, and even Europeans as *Nikmaq,* or kinsmen. Generally, they refer to the tribes or the entire people as *Lnu'k,* or "the People."

The Mi'kmaq consider themselves to be members of one large extended family, and their manner of greeting one another can often lead outsiders to mistakenly believe that they are all indeed blood relatives. Children address their elders as "aunt" or "uncle" and, more importantly, no child is ever abandoned. If a child is orphaned or cannot be cared for by a natural parent for any reason, either a childless couple or another couple with children will look after the child and treat that child as their own.[4] Children born out of wedlock are accepted without stigma. Leadership was by merit and selection and was not hereditary. Candidates for any post had to measure up to very demanding standards of intelligence, courage, and wisdom. Leaders who did not perform well were soon replaced; on the other hand, if their skills were satisfactory, they served until death.[5] Competition for the opportunity to serve their people was quite intense; however, in stark contrast to European practice, this was not to gain wealth, power, or prestige, but for the privilege of giving the highest standards of service to their people.[6]

At the time of Earl Henry's forced landing in 1396, the land of the Mi'kmaq, or Mi'kamagi as it is more properly called, was almost completely forested with birch, maple, beech, oak, pine, spruce, and fir.[7] The Mi'kmaq used tree bark in their housing, in canoe construction, and as containers for food. The wood itself was utilized to make tools, lances, and weapons. In the woodlands were natural meadows, open areas scorched by forest fire or created by bog or marshland. Food plants grew there, such as cranberry, blueberry, raspberry, and strawberry, as well as herbs and medicinal plants. Reeds that grew in the marshes were used to make baskets and mats. The animals of the woodlands—bear, moose, porcupine, hare, grouse, and passenger pigeon—were all essential aids to survival for the people.

The Mi'kmaq lands were well watered with rivers, lakes, and a long coastline that provided the people with a vast and seemingly unending supply of food, including clams, mussels, whelks, squid, crab, lobster, flounder, skate shad, salmon, and eels. Like the Vikings and the Orcadians, the Mi'kmaq were equally at home on the water as they were on the land and caught porpoise, sturgeon, swordfish, and small whales. The waterside was a natural haunt of geese and ducks, as well as seals and walrus. In common with all other hunter-gatherer societies, the local inhabitants had an almost encyclopedic knowledge of the lifestyle and reproductive habits of their prey and the seasonal variations in their food supply. Their innately spiritual traditions displayed a reverence for nature and a deep respect for life, living in harmony with the natural world, and they did not delude themselves that they were its masters. They understood that without Mother Earth and her bounty, they could not exist. There was a stark difference in attitude toward the land shown by the Mi'kmaq on

A People of Peace

the one hand and Europeans on the other. The Mi'kmaq venerated the land, lived on it, gave thanks for its bounty, and knew that they inhabited it with all other living creatures.[8] The European concept of "land owner-ship" was completely beyond their comprehension. Like the vast majority of hunter-gatherer societies, they knew that reigning over the Earth was a supreme being and creator, the Great Spirit, who had created all things and was personified in all of them—in the air they breathed, in the rivers, in the forests, in their families, and in their friends and, above all others, in love, compassion, knowledge, and wisdom. The Great Spirit was goodness incarnate, and they had no need to fear it.

Sex among the Mi'kmaq was regarded as a natural and pleasurable act when performed between consenting individuals in private. Acceptance of homosexuality, at a time of European intolerance, was prevalent across most North American peoples. While the Mi'kmaq term *Geenumu Gessalagee* ("He loves men") referred specifically to homosexual men, it was in fact a part of a broader understanding of sexuality as a spiritual identity. Today this principle is more commonly referred to by the catchall term of a person who has "two spirits," male and female energies. It is in modern times used as an expression of acceptance within the LGBTQ com-munities of the native peoples. While European colonists considered that two-spirit people were homosexual, and while the modern usage of the term could describe someone who is homosexual, historically, two-spirit people did not identify as either homosexual or heterosexual. Two-spirit people did not necessarily see themselves as homosexual, as sexual rela-tionships between consenting adults were understood as a spiritual act, not within today's context of defined sexualities.[9] Native peoples saw two-spirit individuals as being blessed by spiritual intervention in the form of visions and dreams. With this in mind, two-spirit people often filled spiri-tual roles such as healers, shamans, keepers of traditions, and storytellers within their communities. It is only after the introduction of the prose-lytizing Western religious orders that came after Columbus, such as the Catholic and later Mormon churches, which have had little good to say about homosexuality, that intolerance within native peoples begins to be documented.

The Mi'kmaq also took great exception to inappropriate sexual advances being made to wives and daughters but had no concept of any racial barriers between them and people of other races. This was a reflection of a much deeper level of tolerance for the Mi'kmaq. They extended this tolerance to all they met and, with their own democratic forms and relationships, treated all people as being equal. No racial intolerance, no class barriers, no racial or religious prejudice distorted their treatment of other people. They welcomed visitors and settlers alike for "how can one refuse to share the bounties of Mother Earth."[10] The Native American people undoubtedly lagged far behind their European counterparts in technology, engineering, and building, for example; however, in the things that really matter, they far exceeded the Europeans. An innate respect for nature and for all life; a strong sense of community; a dedication to service to others without reward; respect for tribal elders and a democratic system that encouraged every voice in the tribe to speak and be heard—these are standards that we in the West have yet to attain. The word of a Mi'kmaq was that person's bond, and when he entered into a treaty on behalf of his people, he honored it scrupulously—which put him at a severe disadvantage when dealing with the British colonial administration that used and abused every treaty they ever signed, using them as vehicles for slow genocide.[11]

This unspoiled way of life, with its gentle discipline that ruled by diplomacy and persuasion rather than by force, was not merely in harmony with nature but also promoted and encouraged real brotherhood among the people. It spawned a society in which all were valued, an inclusive system where mutual respect, a sense of belonging, and harmony were the norm. Nature dictated its gentle rhythm, and tribal custom looked after the minutiae of daily life. In these matters, the Mi'kmaq were far from unique, since similar customs and traditions pervaded nearly all the other tribes and nations of the Native American people.

The vast majority of the Native American nations did not employ writing as Europeans knew it; they did instead have a means of communication using symbols that, while it produced no literature, developed a considerable level of sophistication. The Mi'kmaq had developed this form

A People of Peace

of record keeping much further than most and used a well-developed and highly sophisticated form of hieroglyphics that poses puzzling questions as to its true origins and earlier contact between ancient Egypt and North America that no one can prove. According to one expert, Nigel Davies:

> A single language cannot be born twice; a linguistic group must have one place of origin and one only, regardless of its subsequent spread. Thus, if two languages, current in two widely separated regions, can be shown to belong to the same family, then a close connection existed between the ancestors of their respective speakers.[12]

If this is true for the spoken word, how much more it must apply to the highly complex and intricate forms of symbolism such as the Egyptian hieroglyphics. When hieroglyphics that are so close in form and meaning are used by two separate and distinct cultures separated by many thousands of miles and years, yet use a similar language, Davies's words begin to ring true. One absolutely incredible theory floated to explain this anomaly claims that French missionaries taught the Mi'kmaq how to use hieroglyphics when they evangelized the nation in 1610. Britain assumed control of Nova Scotia in 1713, so how could French missionaries have taught the Mi'kmaq hieroglyphics between 1610 and 1713 when no one in Europe was able to understand them until after Champollion finally deciphered the Rosetta Stone in 1822? This question will remain unanswered until mainstream American academics grasp the nettle and thoroughly investigate all probable contacts between the Old World and the New in the centuries and millennia prior to 1492.

Part of the problem of investigating pre-Columbian voyages to America arises not from academic-blinkered thinking or prejudice, but from previous writers who, in fits of misplaced enthusiasm, have "over-egged the pudding" and strayed from the pathway of demonstrable fact into the realms of fantasy. We both, Martin and Wallace-Murphy, like facts and, wherever possible, check and then double-check them. The controversy over the Mi'kmaq flag is a case in point. Wallace-Murphy attended the Sinclair Symposium in Kirkwall in Orkney in late 1997. Our party had stopped in Edinburgh a few days previously to visit Rosslyn Chapel, and while we were there, we met a local journalist and friend called John Ritchie. When he saw the Mi'kmaq flag, he claimed he had seen it before, which he had. It had been shown in a painting reproduced in an illustrated book called *The Chronicle of the Crusades*. The flag was flying above a ship supposedly taking King Louis IX of France to the Crusades. Ritchie jumped to the conclusion that the flag was Templar and made quite a fuss about it. We knew that it was not but, knowing Ritchie, set out to verify our assumptions before starting a verbal battle. However, another writer took Ritchie's word as gospel and published that in a book about the St. Clair voyage, in complete contradiction to our comments when he sought our advice. We knew at a gut level that the flag was not Templar. Nor did King Louis travel to Egypt in Templar ships; a Genoese fleet transported him. The flag was a royal flag of France, and it was a party of French missionaries who first evangelized the Mi'kmaq. No Templar connection at all.

A similar problem arises with some of Frederick Pohl's work. Most of his ideas are well worth study and examination, but his conclusions about the alleged relationship between Earl Henry and the hero of the Mi'kmaq creation myth, Glooscap (a legendary figure among some Native peoples), are overimaginative from start to finish. His claims that there are seventeen "identical" correspondences between Glooscap of the legend and Earl Henry St. Clair stretch the bounds of credulity too far and should be dismissed out of hand. The Glooscap legend should be treasured for what it really is—the creation mythology of the Mi'kmaq people. Henry was indeed recorded in oral tradition, for it has been claimed that a secret story is handed down to the Grand Chief on his appointment. This states that when Earl Henry returned to Europe, he took at least one of the Mi'kmaq with him as his guest and this person was returned to his people within a year. This story indicates that this person crossed the Atlantic at least twice. This story was first brought to public notice at a meeting of the *Society De Sancto Claro* in Chicago during the exposition there in 1893. Mention was also made of Earl Henry's time among the Mi'kmaq by the poet Dame Rita Joe, a gifted and courageous lady, at a ceremony in Guysborough to welcome the Italian yachtswoman Laura Zolo, who had just recreated the Zeno/St. Clair voyage from Venice, via Orkney to Guysborough. Part of Dame Rita Joe's celebratory poem can be found in *Templars in America*.

The Mi'kmaq, in common with many other oral cultures, have a finely developed sense of history that lies at the very core of their sense of identity as a people. The Mi'kmaq historian Daniel Paul has written a scathing indictment of the callous brutalities of colonial rule over his people in his masterwork *We Were Not the Savages*. It is a superb history of the survival of a people and a culture against near impossible odds. Therefore, it has been enlightening to see the lengths that this proud nation has gone to in order to participate in the recent celebrations of Earl Henry's original voyage in 1396. They kindly sent several representatives to the Sinclair Symposium in 1997, have contributed to every event in Canada, and have given generously of their time and effort in the ongoing historical research into this momentous voyage. Why is this? Why did Earl Henry relate so well to them? Both Henry and the Zeno family were long-term adherents of the Templar tradition that, like the Native American culture, stressed service to the community as a whole rather than the acquisition of power and wealth for selfish reasons.

CHAPTER 13

The Voyage to Vinland

Oh, farmers, pray that your summers
be wet and your winters clear.

—VIRGIL

Various claims have been made by previous authors that Henry spent a prolonged period of time in this part of the New World after making his first landfall, but all the Zeno Narrative tells us is that he settled down in the harbor and explored the whole of the country as well as both sides of Greenland.[1] It is almost certain that the Zeno/St. Clair party spent about three or, at most, four months deepening their relationship with the Mi'kmaq, investigating the possibilities of trade and the explorations mentioned in the preceding chapter.[2] A petroglyph found at Lilly Lake near Halifax, Nova Scotia, may confirm Henry's presence there. A medieval style shield has been inscribed on a rock on a rocky outcrop in a clearing. Above the incised shield is the Roman numeral IV. The top-left quarter of the shield is inscribed with an eroded and flattened circular pattern; the top-right quarter displays a "sun in splendor" with eight rays; there is a crescent moon in the lower-left quadrant and a stylized variation on the Templar croix pattée in the lower-right quarter. Some of the archaeologists who have studied this carving have remarked that there are similarities between its symbolism and another petroglyph we will discuss later, namely that of the Westford Knight.

The Zeno Narrative informs us that Henry "noticed that the place had a wholesome and pure atmosphere, a fertile soil and good rivers and so many other attractions, he conceived the idea of staying there and founding a city." We have no evidence that he did so; indeed, all the indications are that he did not have sufficient time. The party had arrived in late May, and the Narrative discloses that he ordered the bulk of his fleet to return to Orkney at the beginning of autumn in order to arrive home before winter set in. One of Antonio's letters recounts that "he therefore retained only the oared boats and chose people who were willing to stay with him and sent the rest away in the ships. He appointed me, against my will, to be their captain."[3] The return voyage to Orkney took about twenty-eight days. When Frederick Pohl wrote that Henry kept only a small party with him equipped with small rowing boats, he was once more in the realms of fantasy. No good leader would take such a risk, and Pohl has forgotten the key qualification for using both the Orkney galley and the Venetian galley—like Viking ships of old, they could travel against the wind, an essential quality when sailing against strong southwesterly winds. Pohl's nightmarish idea that Henry built a ship from scratch using green and unseasoned wood in the depths of a Canadian winter and then sailed it down the Bay of Fundy, which has one of the strongest tidal rips in the world, simply demonstrates his lack of any real seafaring experience. We all owe a great deal to Frederick Pohl for bringing the St. Clair voyage to public notice; but when he erred, he did so in a grand manner. I (Wallace-Murphy) am not alone in this view: Colin Clarke, a professional surveyor from Waverley, Nova Scotia, does not believe that Henry would have been so foolish as to send all his ships back to Orkney and rely on building one to make his return. Clarke, who once worked as a shipwright, is quite spicy in his comments and declared that he found Pohl's scenario quite preposterous: "Henry was here to explore, not to build ships, and, even if he did have the tools with him, where did he plan to find dry wood for the construction?"[4]

It is almost certain that, when Earl Henry ordered the bulk of his fleet to return to Orkney, the Venetian galley, which after all was the property of Antonio Zeno, and the small barks were the ships that returned. That would leave Henry with the Orkney galley to continue his explorations. This galley, somewhat smaller than its Venetian counterpart, was also powered by both oars and sail and gave the earl all the flexibility and security he needed. Furthermore, there is one archaeological artifact that tends to support this—the "boatstone" kept on display in the J. V. Fletcher Memorial Library in Westford, Massachusetts.

Henry's voyage in search of Norumbega in Vinland would have replicated those described in the Viking sagas, rounding Cape Trin, gaining considerable sea room, and rowing to the southwest in the teeth of the prevailing wind. While directions for finding Vinland were reasonably accurate, finding Norumbega itself was a different kettle of fish indeed. The settlement had been founded by the Knutson expedition, from which there were few survivors; however, Henry had an ace in the hole in his friends among the Mi'kmaq, part of the Algonquin Confederacy in whose territory Norumbega had been founded. The oral tradition of Henry's allies reports that he took several tribesmen with him to act as guides, interpreters, and emissaries.[5]

The geography of the New England coastal plain is largely flat, and the few hills found there are good vantage points for any exploratory vision. It is on one such place, Prospect Hill near the present-day town of Westford, that we can find evidence that links us indisputably with the St. Clair voyage of 1396. As there are no documentary records of this aspect of Henry's exploration, our reconstruction depends on knowledge of his objectives: archaeological evidence where it occurred, fleshed out by reasoned analysis and Mi'kmaq oral tradition.

The Westford Knight

The petroglyph known as "The Westford Knight" was hardly known for many years and has been a subject for real debate for only the last sixty or more years. A depiction in stone of a medieval knight in full armor, complete with sword and shield on a rocky ledge by a busy road at Westford, Massachusetts, lay unnoticed for centuries. Its first public mention was in a book published in 1883 by the Rev. Edwin R. Hodgman, who wrote:

> A broad ledge which crops near the house of William Kittredge, had upon its surface grooves made by glacier in some far-off geological age. Rude outlines of the human face have been traced upon it and the work is said to be that of Indians.[6]

The attribution in the late nineteenth century as "the work of Indians" is hardly surprising for any artifact that may predate the colonial era. The ledge was examined by Malcolm Pearson and William B. Goodwin in the early 1940s. In 1946, Goodwin wrote a book called *The Ruins of Great Ireland in New England* that was illustrated by photographs, including one of the Westford carving taken by his colleague, Malcolm Pearson. The text described that part of the carving represented a broken sword, an old Viking symbol for a dead warrior. Goodwin was a director of the Wadsworth Atheneum of Hartford, Connecticut.

However, Frank Glynn, the president of the Connecticut Archaeological Society and a graduate of Wesleyan University, made the truly ground-breaking breakthrough in the study of this petroglyph. Glynn made numerous contributions to a variety of archaeological journals through-out the world, but it is his work on the Westford Knight that has ensured his reputation. After many attempts to locate this carving, he was stimulated to continue by his colleague and correspondent, T. C. Lethbridge, another author of extensive works on archaeology.[7] Lethbridge was at that time the director of excavations for the Cambridge (UK) Antiquarian Society and had served over thirty years as a director of the Cambridge University Museum of Archaeology and Anthropology. Not exactly an amateur. After some pressure from Lethbridge, Glynn visited Malcolm Pearson, who informed him that the carving had been destroyed during road widening. This error was not resolved until May 1954, when Glynn was directed to the carving. With the skilled assistance of Malcolm Pearson, a series of both black-and-white and color photographs were taken. The carving consisted of a series of peck marks made with an armorer's chisel that delineated the figure, and the photographs were taken by applying chalk to each of them. The chalk highlighted the peck marks in such a manner that the outline of a tall knight in medieval armor draped in a long surcoat was outlined on the rock. In the center was a long pommel sword that ran from the figure's lower thorax to his feet. The shape of a helmet can also be seen surmounted by a birdlike design and, on the knight's left arm, a shield.

Glynn wrote a letter to Lethbridge, enclosing the photographs, and received a reply in which the Englishman wrote:

> Well done! . . . A medieval knight holding a sword . . . the whole thing never, more than outlined and, perhaps not completed because something happened. . . . I expect that you will be burnt at the stake for finding something pre-Columbian, but it is worth it. I don't see how it can be anything but European Medieval.[8]

Glynn soon summoned A. J. Gagne and E. R. Beauchop, curators at the John W. Higgins Armory, to visit the site. Their study of the helmet convinced them of the carving's authenticity, as it was typical of a year somewhere between 1376 and 1400. They also spotted a "saucy little rampant lion on the round pommel." At their suggestion, Glynn then submitted the question of the arms depicted on the shield to the Lord Lyon King of Arms in Edinburgh. His reply was that similar shields were known from the Elgin-Inverness region during the fourteenth century and that maybe the knight in question could have been a "de l'Ard" or "Sperre" and requested some enlarged photos for further study.

Lethbridge suggested that the carving was within fifty years of 1350 and was more like a memorial brass rather than a Templar grave marker. In a later letter, Lethbridge put his finger on the crux of the matter when he wrote: "Either I am quite gaga or we have got this thing solved. No one will believe it of course . . . your knight should be some relative of the Sinclairs."[9]

Lethbridge kept up his investigation of the coat of arms in Europe and eventually submitted his queries to the "Unicorn Herald," Sir Iain Moncreiffe of that Ilk. Sir Iain responded with the following letter:

> The 14th century Knight in Massachusetts is absolutely fascinating, and his heraldry certainly seems to point to the Scottish noble families of Norse origin, though it looks pretty crude, and I wonder if Mr Glynn has traced it quite right on his surcoat. A galley would never be on a knight's shield to signify "journeys end!" His shield would only bear his ancestral coat of arms. In Scotland galleys fall into two main groups: (1) the galley, usually black, born by descendants in the male or female line of Norse kings of the Isles . . . such as the MacDonalds, Campbells, MacDougalls, Macleods, Macleans, Stewarts of Appin etc and (2) the galley, usually gold, born by descendants in the male or female line of the Norse Jarls of Orkney (the family of Rognvald the Wise) such as the Sinclairs or St Clairs . . . the figure's costume and sword together with the galley on his shield, all fit so happily into the context of Jarl Henry's expedition, that I'd be very surprised if it wasn't from one of his companions.[10]

The Unicorn Herald's precision was such that there can be no more realistic argument about the Wexford Knight's origins or authenticity. Further study of the armorial designs on the shield convinced him that they were "the armorial bearings for a Clan Gunn chief from Thurso," namely, "Gules a lymph ad, sails furled, oars in saltire and in chief a mullet Gold between two buckles Silver." Later he put the matter beyond all doubt, for when he was told of academia's habit of howling fraud or forgery, he dismissed even the remote possibility of that charge sticking with the simple statement that "only three other people in the world, other than himself, would have the knowledge to depict these fourteenth century armorial bearings with such precision or know enough about late medieval armour to fake a carving such as that in Massachusetts."[11] Thus, it is almost certain that the

Westford Knight is a memorial to Sir James Gunn, a close friend and companion of Earl Henry St. Clair.

The connection between the carving and the St. Clair/Zeno voyage was stressed by Sir Iain Moncreiffe in the following words:

> [T]he effigy of a fourteenth century knight in bassinet, camail and surcoat, with a heater-shaped shield bearing devices of a Norse-Scottish character such as might have been expected of a knight in Jarl Sinclair's entourage, and a pommel sword of that period is hardly likely to be a coincidence. I rather think that the mighty Jarl stayed awhile—possibly wintered in Massachusetts.[12]

The effigy was punched into the rock by an armorer, as materials for a traditional brass were simply not available. Examination of the punch marks by the American archaeologist Jim Whittall demonstrates that the metal punch used to make the effigy had grown progressively more blunt as the incisions progressed. Two other archaeologists, Austin Hildreth and H. J. Omara, did a comparative study of similar incisions on early gravestones and concluded that the punch marks on the Westford carving were in the region of 500 to 800 years old.[13]

The Boatstone

Investigations were then initiated to try to locate the earl's winter camp in line with Sir Iain's comments mentioned earlier. Frederick Pohl joined Glynn in this search, and they were shown an inscribed stone that had been found by a local farmer. It shows a ship with a single mast with two sails and also eight ports for oars. Besides the carving of the ship are an arrow and the numeral 184. Near to where it was found were three stone enclosures similar to the old Viking buildings in Greenland known as "stor-houses."[14] The depiction of an oared sailing boat on this stone tends to confirm our theory that Henry used an Orkney galley for this part of his voyage. However, pending further archaeological excavation, the so-called stor-houses, while a possible site for the expedition's winter quarters, cannot be held to be a proof of this theory. The boatstone now is on permanent exhibition at the J. V. Fletcher Memorial Library in Westford, Massachusetts.

Sadly, the exposed position of the Westford Knight, immediately adjacent to a busy road and subject to almost constant water erosion, has led to an inevitable deterioration of the carving. However, the early photographs taken by Malcolm Pearson, Jim Whittall, and Frank Glynn have left us with a permanent record of the site before pollution started its decay. Niven Sinclair commissioned a rubbing to be made by Marianna Lines in 1991. She used traditional brass rubbing techniques using wax and a mixture of floral and vegetable juices. The results were astounding and revealed the complex nature of the carving in a startling manner. Since then, a chain-link fence suspended from stone pillars has fenced off the carving. A plaque explaining the history of the effigy and the story of Henry's voyage and his relationship with Sir James Gunn has also been installed.[15] An act of criminal desecration was committed that contaminates this important site, however; some well-intentioned vandal has painted over the armorial bearings on the shield.

The urgent matter of the preservation of this site has been virtually ignored despite gaining agreement in principle for this from the Archaeological Commissioners of the Commonwealth of Massachusetts. Our good friend Niven Sinclair, Norman Biggart, Malcolm Pearson, and Wallace-Murphy made a presentation to them in the autumn of 1999. Malcolm Pearson presented a letter from the consultant geologist Joseph A. Sinnot who wrote this about the carving:

> After a lengthy and detailed study of the rock outcropping in the field it is my opinion that a pecked and etched image of an historical event has been emplaced on the bedrock. . . . Natural or glacial markings such as striations, grooves, polishing and weathering are all apparent on the rock, but do not diminish the stature of the image placed there at a much later date. I have been the State Geologist for Massachusetts for twenty-two years . . . and also the Director of The Massachusetts

Underwater Archaeology Board for five years and understand the commission's desire for authenticity . . . the etching is solidly and authentically placed on the bedrock and deserves preservation.[16]

Agreement was reached in principle to preserve the carving, but sadly, lack of funds continues to delay its proper and permanent protection. Yet, despite this recognition and the clearly expressed professional opinions of an impressive list of experts in their field as to the authenticity of the carving, we are only too well aware that the majority of academic historians in the USA will still refuse to credit that anyone from Europe reached America before Columbus. But, to any open-minded and serious student of our common history, the evidence and expert opinion are overwhelming and demonstrate that Earl Henry St. Clair reached the shores of America and traveled inland over a century before the fateful voyage of Christopher Columbus.

CHAPTER 14

The Most Controversial Building in North America

*Time crumbles things; everything grows old under the
power of time and is forgotten through the lapse of time.*

—ARISTOTLE

Without doubt, the most controversial structure on the North American continent is the one known as the Old Stone Mill at Newport, Rhode Island—more simply as the Newport Tower. Regarding the nature of this building, if this circular rubble-built tower with its eight supporting pillars were located in Europe, it would be dated to the twelfth to fourteenth centuries without causing the slightest ripple of concern among academics.[1] This stone tower, which is surrounded by a wrought iron fence in a public park, is truly an architectural anachronism. The controversy over its true age and origin has been prolonged and strident, to the extent that makes the *odium theologicum* of the doctrinal disputes of the early Christian Church seem like squabbles in a kindergarten.

The architectural style and the manner of the building's construction prove, beyond all dispute, that the Newport Tower was not built by the Native American people of the area or by those who built in stone in

Central or South America. According to Professor Eben Norton Horsford of Harvard, the Newport Tower has the shape form of a baptistery, and he believes that it indicates a Viking presence in Newport that pre-dates the colonial era by several centuries.[2] In this, he is echoing the comments made in 1879 by R. G. Hatfield, the president of the New York chapter of the American Institute of Architects, who claimed that the tower was built by the original founders of the Vinland colony, namely the Vikings.[3] The professor of medieval architecture at Harvard in 1954, Kenneth J. Conant, said of this controversial structure: "The actual fabric is medieval while the statistics of the building are Norse. It so happens that the only arch left from Medieval Norse construction in Greenland is like that."[4] He is later reported to have said in reference to the window and doorway of the first floor of the tower: "The semi-circle and discharging arch and tympanum are regular medieval construction, carried down from classical times and lost sight of by colonial times."[5] The structural engineer Edward Adams Richardson of Bethlehem, Pennsylvania, believed that the tower itself could be questioned to provide information on when it was built. Writing in 1960, he claimed, "The design process adequate, by modern standards, for a particular structure, while the windows and fireplace form a sophisticated signalling and ship guidance system characteristic of the 14th century."[6] According to Hjalmar Holand: "As even a small cannon would be sufficient enough to destroy the tower, this implies that it was built before 1400, when cannons came into general use."[7]

> [I]t is one of the least impressive structures you ever saw [the Newport Tower] . . . For more than a century now, an occasionally scholarly, often fantastic, usually bitter dispute has ranged about this round tower. Over 100 books, articles and pamphlets have attempted to throw light on its origin and purpose. The Irish, the Portuguese, the Dutch and even the ancient Druids have been suggested as the builders; but there have been only two theories that hold water—the Norse and the Colonial.[8]

That is the view of one architect with an interest in history, but there are far more than two theories as to who built the tower, and all the controversy proves is that whatever view is taken, it will doubtless be championed by men of unswerving conviction and, in reality, merely indicates how little is known about the tower.[9]

The building is almost circular with an outer diameter of just over 7 meters. It stands about 8 meters above ground level and is supported by eight round pillars that are linked by Romanesque arches. The arches rest on cylindrical stone-built pillar bases that were originally visible and would have added nearly half a meter to the height of each pillar.[10] The inside surface of the pillars is flush with the inner surface of the walls they support, while their outside surfaces project about 25 centimeters from the outer sides of the walls.[11] The top of each pillar is marked by a thin sloping stone or slate slab that projects at an angle.[12] The inside of the circular wall is marked by post holes that once housed substantial beams, and there are also three window openings, several small peepholes, a built-in fireplace with two flues, faint traces of steps, and several niches of varying sizes.[13] According to Sue Carlson, an architect working for New England Historical Restorations, writing in 1997:

> To all trained architects and architectural historians, the style of the Tower is unquestionably medieval, as indicated by the quality of the rough stone masonry with its round stone columns supporting stone arches awkwardly making a transition to the superstructure above.[14]

The idea that the Newport Tower may well have been a baptistery or church gains some credence when it is compared to Great Heddinge Church in Denmark, St. Olaf's Church at Tønsberg in Norway, the Church of St. Mikael in Schleswig in Denmark, Østerlars Church and Ole-Kirke on Bornholm (see below), Vårdsberg Church in Östergötland in Sweden, the Church of the Holy Sepulchre in Cambridge, England, or the plans of the round church that once stood at Nidaros in Norway.[15] Another round church surrounded by the ruin of a roofed ambulatory can be found at

Lanleff in Brittany, but this round church stands on ten columns rather than eight. Circular churches with octagonal sacred geometry were built throughout Europe by the Templars;[16] some of these churches can be found on the Danish island of Bornholm in the Baltic.

Every architect who has commented on the Newport Tower describes its design and structure as medieval, and whether it was built as a church, lighthouse, or mill, it is unquestionably pre-Columbian in date. European architects, historians, and archaeologists, who are not subject to the same rigid and dogmatic constraints as their American colleagues, are unanimous in their belief that the tower is of medieval and European design. Professor Charles Rafn, who held the chair in the department of Northern Antiquities in Denmark, "suggested that the tower was a Norse Christian baptistery."[17] Four renowned authorities in art and early archaeology—Professors Boiseree, Klenze, Tiersch, and Kalenbach—recorded their views in the following terms: "Judging from drawings of the Old Stone Mill sent from America, having all declared in favour of the ruin being the remains of a baptismal chapel in the early style of the Middle Ages." The Danish historian Johannes Brønsted wrote in 1951: "The medievalisms are so conspicuous that, if the tower were in Europe, dating it to the Middle Ages would probably meet with no protest." The Swedish architectural historian Hugo Frolen said that the tower was Anglo-Norman in design and compared it to the Templar churches in both Northampton and Cambridge mentioned earlier. Dr. F. J. Allen, an English architectural historian, wrote in 1921 that the Newport Tower was "of the shape and central portion of a 12th century round church from which the surrounding aisle or ambulatory has been removed."[18] Some American academics seem to have broken ranks and are in seeming agreement with their European colleagues. The Board of Regents of the Smithsonian Institution said, "[E]verything taken into consideration we are most inclined to regard the Newport Tower as an English watchtower or beacon."[19] American independent historian and author Gunnar Thompson notes that in respect of the tower, "[W]e do find a similar technique in medieval buildings in the Scottish Isles."[20] On the other hand, Haraldur Sigurðsson of the University of Rhode Island, after a prolonged examination of the tower, claimed that it was unlikely to be either Viking in origin or built before 1200 CE because of the presence of ancient mortar. Nonetheless, in his opinion, it had been built to Scandinavian design. In light of the fervor with which many local historians and residents put the case for the tower being of early colonial construction, it may be of interest to list the earliest mention of the tower from both archival and cartographical sources.

Pre-Colonial References to the Tower

When the Italian explorer Verrazzano, who was, incidentally, working for the French, landed in Narragansett Bay in 1524, he described a European-style structure located on the east side of the bay near its mouth, which he called a Norman villa.[21] He described the people near the tower as the most beautiful and civilized that he had met on his expedition; they were larger than his own people, and he called them "white European-Amer-Norse."[22] When the first English settlers arrived in this district in the 1600s, they described a group of fair-haired and blue-eyed natives as "the banished Indians" who may have been descendants of the people described by Verrazzano.[23]

There are several early maps in which a building or settlement of some description is marked on the site of Newport, Rhode Island. In Mercator's world map, published in 1569, the tower was clearly recorded and placed in present-day New England, which the geographer called, intriguingly, Norumbega.[24] Another, made by the Dutchman Cornelius Hendrickson before 1614, was later included in his atlas, published in 1635. The original map, found in the Dutch archives of The Hague in 1841,[25] shows the island and coast of Narragansett Bay, the one small area on the side of the bay marked "New England," the only part of the map with an English name. On this map, a "Toret" is shown as a small circle on the western end of Newport Island.[26]

The Englishman John Smith left a description of this area and a chart of its coast, dated 1614, that accurately charts Narragansett Bay, Mount Hope Bay, and Mount Hope and its Indian village. When passing the site of Newport, Smith spied some structure there, which he believed was an English settlement, and marked the site on his map.[27] Later, in 1621, he received a letter

The Most Controversial Building in North America

from "New Plymouth" describing the new colony. Apparently, when he marked this position on his chart, he renamed the original site that he had indicated as "an English settlement" as "Old Plymouth."[28]

It was described as a "rownd stone towr" by English seafarers in 1629–1630,[29] and William Wood mentioned it on a map he derived from coastal observation in 1629. According to Arlington H. Mallery, writing in 1958, Wood's belief that there was an English settlement on the site of Newport in 1629 was not inspired by a map, but by his own sightings of the Newport Tower.[30]

In London, records exist of a petition in 1632 by Sir Edmund Plowden[31] to establish a colony on Rhode Island that was to be called "New Albion" and later became known as "Old Plymouth." In this petition, he describes an existing round tower as an asset for the colony.[32] Neither Sir Edmund nor his heirs ever exploited their successful petition, but a colony was eventually founded in 1636, and the city of Newport in 1639.[33] The tower is mentioned in a deed dated 1642, which states that the boundary line of the property is "so many lots from the Old Stone Tower."[34] According to Benson J. Lossing, it was there when the English settlers came, and he believed that the natives had no knowledge to its origin,[35] although we have since learned that the elders of the Narragansett Indians have a tradition that stated the tower was constructed by "green-eyed, fire-haired giants who came in peace, had a battle and then left."[36] So, apart from the oral tradition of the local Native American people, there are eight cartographical or archival references to the tower that all predate colonial settlement.

Who Built the Tower? Conflicting Theories

The city of Newport, Rhode Island, was founded in 1639, yet in a document dated 1642, the tower was referred to as "The Old Stone Tower." Therefore, it is reasonable to assume that the tower is older than the city in which it now stands. A later governor of Rhode Island, Benedict Arnold, arrived in the city in or about 1653, and the tower is mentioned in his will as "the old stone wind miln."[37] On the basis of this brief reference, a nonsensical theory has been founded that defies both logic and fact—one that claims that Governor Benedict Arnold built the tower as a windmill. This pathetic theory steadfastly ignores the recorded facts that, firstly, the tower pre-dated the foundation of the city; secondly, that it is mentioned in a report dated some eleven years before Arnold arrived there. The simplest rebuttal of this nonsense came in 1811 when the American historian George G. Channing wrote:

> The problem concerning the origin and purpose of this ancient structure is no nearer solution than it was two hundred years and more ago. Speculation of all sorts with regard to it, both here and abroad, have nearly died out; and notwithstanding the allusion in an ancient deed to the ownership of the land, "my stone mill standing thereon" it has never been imagined that the aforesaid proprietor had anything to do with the construction of this unique pile of stone and mortar. The very nature and grace of the structure preclude the idea that it could have been erected upon almost barren waste merely to grind Indian corn to powder. Not a vestige of any similar edifice has been seen on the continent. The notion that Indian sagacity might, without a precedent, have wrought such a massive and artistic work Is taxing credulity unwarrantably.[38]

Channing is far from alone in his skepticism, and a more recent publication echoes the same theme:

> There is a strong probability amounting almost to a certainty that the English colonists found the tower here when they landed and that Governor Arnold modified it to serve the purposes of a windmill.[39]

The new settlers' need for a mill to grind corn is not disputed; however, when one was built, it was recorded, and the first such noteworthy construction was celebrated in 1663. This mill was made entirely of wood and its location precisely noted. Realistically, despite its description as a windmill, the Newport Tower is completely unsuitable for such a purpose. Firstly, it is not sufficiently circular to have a revolving top to catch the wind; secondly, the eight pillars could not sustain the pressure of the mill mechanism in action, much less the vibrations that would ensue. Historian Benson J. Lossing summed up the fatuity of proponents of the mill theory when he wrote:

> Its form, its great solidarity and its construction upon columns, forbid the idea that it was originally erected for a mill; and certainly if a common windmill made of timber was so highly esteemed by the people, as we have seen, the construction of such an edifice, so superior to any dwelling or church in the colony, would have received special attention from the magistrates and historians of the day.[40]

We are forced to the conclusion that despite being referred to as a mill, the Newport Tower—owing to the nature of its construction—could never have been used for such a purpose.

Another theory for the origins of the tower claims that it is a relic of the Viking settlement of Vinland, and its supporters are just as vehement, illogical, and impervious to reason as those of the Benedict Arnold school. They completely ignore the comment of Dr. Haraldur Sigurðsson of the University of Rhode Island, cited earlier, that the Vikings of that era did not use mortar in their stone constructions.

A third theory, one that has some degree of plausibility and logic, was proposed by Dr. Manuel Luciano da Silva, who was a physician at the Bristol County Medical Center in Rhode Island. He wrote, in a medical journal no less, that the design of the Newport Tower resembled, in its design at least, the rotunda of the old Templar monastery of Tomar in Portugal. Now, as we mentioned previously, round churches were indeed built by the Templars in various parts of Europe and were based on the design of the Church of the Holy Sepulchre in Jerusalem. The monastery at Tomar was originally built as the headquarters of the order in Portugal and later became the central command post for the Knights of Christ, who succeeded them after their suppression. The central part of the monastery, the rotunda is firmly based on octagonal Templar sacred geometry, as is the Newport Tower. The third Grandmaster of the Knights of Christ was Prince Henry the Navigator, who sent two knights of the order, Gaspar and Miguel Corte-Real, to Narragansett Bay to evangelize the natives. They are said to have spent nine years there, which, if they had skilled building help, was certainly enough time to construct the tower.[41] Da Silva was completely dismissive of the colonial theory for the origin of the tower, as he claimed that "the feeble locking columns of the Newport Tower could never sustain the tremors and stresses of use as a windmill." He cast aside the Viking theory as the cryptic, but absolutely accurate, comment that Leif Eriksson could not have been inspired by the Church of the Holy Sepulchre in Jerusalem because the first crusade did not take place until nearly a century after Leif's death.

The final theory that we will put forward is that the Newport Tower was built by the St. Clair/Zeno expedition during the course of one of their two voyages to North America. We will demonstrate the proof of this after recounting the often-controversial results of a variety of historical, scientific, and archaeological examinations of the tower.

A Skeleton in the Closet?

It is worth noting that in the general vicinity of the Newport Tower, at Fall River, Massachusetts, a "Skeleton in Armor" was discovered by Hannah Borden Cook in May of 1831. Information relating to this intriguing skeleton had come about during my (Martin's) research for a television documentary series, examining an infamous relative of Borden Cook, Lizzie Borden. Borden Cook had found the cadaver while apparently scouring some knives at the shoreline, whereby she discovered a skull and then later a skeleton—apparently not the only Borden to have been associated with sharp objects and a body! The skeleton was exposed and was found to be buried in an unusual position, adorned by a brass breastplate and a quiver of brass arrows. Given that the local Native Americans were not known to have advanced in the field of metallurgy, could this skeleton have hailed from further ashore? An intriguing contemporary account of this skeleton came from John Stark, esquire, a lawyer who found the skeleton to have been

"buried in a sitting posture, the head being about one foot below what had been for many years the surface of the ground." The surrounding earth was carefully removed and the body found to be enwrapped in a covering of coarse bark of a dark colour. Within this envelope were found the remains of another of coarse cloth, made of fine bark and about the texture of a Manilla coffee-bag. On the breast was a plate of brass, thirteen inches long, six broad at the upper end and five at the lower. This plate appears to have been cast and is from one-eighth to three thirty-seconds of an inch in thickness. It is so much corroded that whether or not anything was ever engraved upon it has not yet been ascertained. It is oval in form, the edges being irregular, apparently made so by corrosion.

Below the breastplate, and entirely encircling the body, was a belt composed of brass tubes, each four and a half inches in length and three-sixteenths of an inch in diameter, arranged longitudinally and close together, the length of the tube being the width of the belt. The tubes are of thin brass, cast upon hollow reeds, and were fastened together by pieces of sinew. This belt was so placed as to protect the lower parts of the body below the breastplate. The arrows are of brass, thin, flat, and triangular in shape, with a round hole cut through near the base. The shaft was fastened to the head by inserting the latter in an opening at the end of the wood, and then tying it with a sinew through the round hole, a mode of constructing the weapon never practiced by the Indians, not even with their arrows of thin shell. Parts of the shaft still remain attached to some of them. When first discovered the arrows were in a sort of quiver of bark, which fell in pieces when exposed to the air.

The skull is much decayed, but the teeth are sound and apparently of a young man. The pelvis is much decayed and the smaller bones of the lower extremities are gone.

The integuments of the right knee, for four or five inches above and below, are in good preservation, apparently the size and shape of life, although quite black.

He continued:

That the body was not one of the Indians we think needs no argument. We have seen some of the drawings taken from the sculptures found at Palenque, and in those the figures are represented with the breastplates, although smaller than the plate found at Fall River. On the figures at Palenque the bracelets and anklets seem to be of a manufacture precisely similar to the belt of tubes just described.

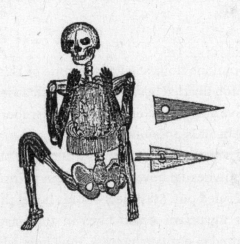

If the body found at Fall River be one of the Asiatic race, who transiently settled in Central America, and afterwards went to Mexico and founded those cities, in exploring the ruins of which such astonishing discoveries have recently been made, then we may well suppose also that it is one of the race whose exploits have, although without a date and almost without a certain name, been immortalized by Homer. Of the great race who founded cities and empires in their eastward march, and are finally lost in South America, the Romans seem to have had a glimmering tradition in the story of Evander.

But we rather incline to the belief that the remains found at Fall River belonged to the crew of a Phoenician vessel. The spot where they were found is on the seacoast, and in the immediate neighbourhood of Dighton Rock, famed for its hieroglyphic inscriptions, of which no sufficient explanation has yet been given, all near which rock brazen vessels have been found. If this latter hypothesis be adopted, a part of it is that these mariners, the unwilling and unfortunate discoverers of a new world, lived sometime after they landed, and having written their names, perhaps their epitaphs, upon the rock at Dighton, died, and were buried by the natives.[42]

A variety of opinions flourished at the time of this discovery as to its origins, with opinion divided between those with a view that the skeleton represented a Native American chief, perhaps a member of the Narragansett or Wampanoag tribe. It is possible that the brass to make the arrowheads had been traded with later European settlers and then at a later date fashioned into arrowheads; however, an origin point from further afield cannot equally be ruled out. Stark sets out his belief that the Phoenicians, Carthaginians, or Egyptians could have in the past discovered North America. As we noted in earlier chapters, the Phoenicians, Carthaginians, and Romans may have routinely navigated the coasts of the northeastern Atlantic, and a vessel, perhaps blown off course, may have reached North America. Given the state of preservation of the skeleton upon discovery, it may lead us to a later date, perhaps of the medieval period, favoring a time frame of the Zeno brothers or of Henry St. Clair. It is with regret that the skeleton is no longer with us to be carbon-dated. The Skeleton had been moved to the Fall River Athenaeum, which subsequently was destroyed by fire in 1843. This said, the area around Newport is no stranger to finds that may predate the Columbian discovery hypothesis.

CHAPTER 15

Dissension, Discussion, and Debate

*Libraries are as the shrine where all the relics of the
ancient saints, full of true virtue, and all that without
delusion or imposture are preserved and restored.*

—SIR FRANCIS BACON

We would love to be in a position to report that strictly scientific archaeological examination of the Newport Tower had settled the debate over its origins once and for all. Sadly, few of the examinations and the subsequent reports on the Tower's provenance have been dispassionate, unbiased, or conclusive. Most of them, in fact, rather than achieving a degree of clarification, indeed have muddied the waters even more. The first archaeological excavation was marred by clearly expressed bias, flawed methodology, and a series of unjustifiable and unwarranted assumptions.

William S. Godfrey gave the game away about his own personal bias both in the title of his dissertation—"Digging a Tower and Laying a Ghost"—and in the opening paragraphs of his final report in which he wrote:

[H]e [Benedict Arnold] purchased some of his Newport property, specifically the section on which **he later built his house**

and the stone mill, the year before he moved. . . . At some period before 1677 **Arnold built the Old Stone Mill** [our emphasis].[1]

Thus, this supposedly dispassionate and analytical archaeologist has already decided who built the mill before his investigation even commences. This conclusion was reached despite a complete lack of paperwork concerning the building in question and without any archaeological evidence to support it. His total bias shows again when he mentions other authors' views on the tower. He writes, "Means reviews the writings on the tower with great care but fails to find any Newporter . . . who had lost his head to the Norse." Godfrey even suggests that an earlier governor of Rhode Island, William Gibbs, had supported the Viking theory purely to gain some political advantage. Was Godfrey not merely a highly flawed and inexperienced archaeology student—his report gained him his PhD—or was he also retrospectively clairvoyant? He dismissed all those who disagreed with his own theories as "crackpots, pygmies, zealots or the lunatic fringe."[2] He states as an indisputable fact that there is absolutely no proof of the existence of the tower until 1677 and deliberately ignores the long list of archival and cartographic references quoted earlier.

Some four years after Godfrey's flawed report, a structural engineer, Arlington Mallery, assisted by two City of Newport engineers, Gardner Easton and John Howieson, re-examined Godfrey's excavations.[3] Mallery was truly dispassionate and made no comment in favor of any of the conflicting theories regarding the origin of the tower; he simply reported exactly what he found in the following terms:

> We also dug plaster from under the bottom stones of the foundation and found that every joint and opening in the foundation was carefully and thoroughly caulked with refill clay containing particles or fragments of plaster to prevent water seepage. Since all of that plaster except possibly a few fragments had to come from the superstructure of the tower, it could not have been placed inside the joints and crevices

of the present foundation unless the foundation had been installed as underpinning after the tower was built.[4]

He continued:

> The tower was probably underpinned in 1675. The quantity of plaster fragments in the excavation indicates that the plaster stucco had so far disintegrated that the tower must have been more than 300 years old when it was underpinned.[5]

Thus, in the opinion of a skilled structural engineer, the tower was, most probably, constructed in the later quadrant of the fourteenth century. No one has, as yet, come up with the slightest bit of credible evidence to refute Mallery's conclusions.

An international team of investigators, led by Jan Heinemeir and Högne Junger, arrived in 1992 to take samples of mortar from the tower for carbon-dating analysis. Eight core samples were taken, one from each pillar, but only those from pillars six and seven were tested for reasons that were not given. The sample taken from the wall of the fireplace at a level of 420 centimeters was rejected for reasons that again were not disclosed. Surface samples were also taken and tested; pillar eight, for example, gave a range of dates running from 1550 until 1770, and another from the chimney flue registered as 1680 to 1810. Two samples from pillar six were tested, and one gave a range of 1750 to 1930; the other from 1510 to 1640. Several of the core samples taken from pillar seven were summarily rejected without reasons given, and four gave a range of dates from 1410 to 1855. This so-called scientific approach satisfied no one and did nothing to clarify the true age of the tower. Are the flaws in this investigation a result of poor methodology, or is the concept of carbon-dating mortar itself highly flawed? One analytical chemist, James L. Guthrie, roundly condemned both the tests and the results in the following terms:

> The plaster dating results of Heinemeir and Junger are not to be taken seriously because of the small number of samples

tested, the poor precision of the methods revealed by the only test run in duplicate and by the unwarranted assumption that all of the mortar and plaster is of the same age. . . . The possibility that any of the specimens was a pure sample of original mortar seems remote. . . . The apparent belief that a single ambiguous result from a nearby 17th century house is an adequate control. . . . Errors, especially the adsorption of modern carbon dioxide would tend to date samples closer to the present than to the date of mixing.[6]

The inherent problem in trying to carbon-date mortar samples arises from the porous nature of mortar and the fact that carbon interchange may continue for perhaps several hundred years; this problem is one that has not been fully addressed. Another point was made by Dr. Alan Watchman, a geological dating expert of Data-Roche Watchman Inc., who wrote of the report on the tower:

The data in table 1 of the article can be used to suggest an age of about 550 radio-carbon years might be obtained from measuring the more acid resistant carbon in the mortar—taking into consideration possible diffusion, particle size, crystallisation and fractionation effects. If my hypothesis is correct the calibrated age for the mortar would be about 1400 AD.[7]

Professor Andre de Bethune, Professor of Chemistry at Boston College, said:

There are serious doubts in my mind concerning the mortar testing at the tower . . . the timing yielded by the tests is close to the time that Governor Arnold . . . referred to the tower in his last will and testament. But does that date truly give as the age of the tower?[8]

Professor de Bethune stated that the date could be valid only if we could be absolutely certain that there had been no further exchange of carbon dioxide between the carbonate in the mortar and atmospheric carbon dioxide. For unlike wood or fiber samples, we can be sure that all carbon dioxide exchange ceases when the tree or plant dies. With porous ionic solids such as mortar, an exchange of carbon dioxide does tend to continue, especially in a damp climate such as Rhode Island. While such gas-solid exchanges are extremely slow, we know that, in this instance, we are dealing with a time scale in excess of 300 years, and this continuing exchange would have "rejuvenated" the mortar, so to speak, in respect of its Carbon-14 content. Professor de Bethune concedes that "an earlier origin for our Newport Tower—Portuguese or Viking—cannot be excluded even in the face of painstaking carbon fourteen analyses."[9] Professor de Bethune was not only emeritus Professor of Chemistry at Boston College but also a close colleague of Professor Willard F. Libby, who first developed carbon-dating techniques.

A colleague and friend of my co-author Wallace-Murphy, the late James P. (Jim) Whittall Jr. of the Early Sites Research Society, made the most thorough comparative study of the tower that has been done to date. Jim had worked as an archaeologist for over twenty-five years prior to his death in 1998, and six-and-a-half years of that was spent working on the Newport Tower. Unlike Godfrey, Whittall spent a considerable amount of time and trouble examining buildings of similar age and construction throughout northern Europe. His meticulous and detailed findings are contained in the Jim Whittall Archive, and while they are far too voluminous to be included here, it is profitable to examine his summary and conclusions.

The Architecture of the Newport Stone Tower

By James P. Whittall, 1997

The Newport Stone Tower in Touro Park, Newport, Rhode Island, was constructed in the style of Norman-Romanesque architecture inspired by the architecture of the Holy Sepulchre in Jerusalem brought back to Europe by returning Crusaders. In its own unique style, the tower was further influenced by a combination of the architecture of temples of the Templars, the round churches of Scandinavia, and local architectural traditions from whence the builders came. Architectural features found within the construction of the tower would date it in the broad range of 1150 to 1400 AD. However, some specific features limit it to a period in the late 1300s. In the course of six years of research I have found the best parallels in the tower's architectural features exist in the Northern Isles of Scotland which were under Norse control in the timeframe mentioned. Other features relating the tower to Scandinavian round churches and Templar buildings have been published by Hjalmar Holand, Philip A. Means and F. J. Allen.

Some of my conclusions to date.
1. The architecture of the tower was pre-planned. The concept was not conceived on site and built in haste.
2. The architecture is completely involved with sacred geometry.
3. The masons were completely familiar with the materials on hand with which to construct the tower.
4. The tower was aligned to the east and each pillar (8) was placed on a cardinal point in the manner of the Templars. It was not constructed using a magnetic compass. Today, designated pillar 1 is 3 degrees west of the North pole star.
5. The tool marks created in the dressing out of the stonework can be directly related to tools manufactured before 1400. These

marks are unique and unknown when compared to tool marks found in colonial stonework.

6. After extensive comparison with ancient units of measurement, we have found that the unit of measurement for the construction of the tower is best suited to the Scottish Ell or the Norwegian Alen. A photogrammetric survey made in 1991 showed that the unit of measurement used for the tower was 23,35 cm, which supports the idea that the Scottish Ell was used in constructing the tower. The English foot wasn't used.

7. The single and double splay windows have prototypes in Medieval Europe and the Northern Isles of Scotland in the 1300s and in the bishop's palace in Orkney.

8. The arch and lintel design noted in the tower is to be found in Orkney, Shetland and Scandinavian church architecture before 1400.

9. I have found, in extensive research, that the triangle keystone feature of the arches of the tower only seem to have been found in buildings in Orkney, Shetland, Greenland (4 examples), and to a very limited degree in other buildings in the Scottish Isles (3) and in Ireland (2).

10. Built-in niches in the tower have parallel examples in Medieval construction in Orkney and Shetland. Features basically unknown in New England architecture except in some post 1700 stone chambers.

11. The plinth, pillars, capital, arch architecture of the tower has no prototype in New England Colonial architecture, yet it is found in Kirkwall in Orkney.

12. The design of the fireplace with its double flue dates to the 1300s and was out of fashion after the 1400s. There are prototypes of this design in Scotland. Research has indicated the probability that the fireplace and its relationship to the west-facing window was used as a lighthouse and probably signal station. The same can be said for the windows on the third level.

13. The walls were covered with a plaster stucco finish both exterior and interior. Stucco finishing started in the 1200s and is a feature known in Orkney and Scotland.
14. The probable layout and design of the floor joists with corbels has parallels in Medieval Scotland.
15. Probable first floor entry by ladder through the window/entry 3 is a trait found in the Round Churches of Scandinavia.
16. Some architectural features in the tower have been organised to utilise astronomical alignments as a calendar event. Some of the alignments fall on Holy Days of the Norse and Knights Templar. There are prototypes in northern Europe.
17. Probability of an ambulatory around the tower (planned for but not necessarily built); examples in Templar construction and round churches.
18. The tower is located approximately the same latitude as Rome. This would make it an ideal reference point for exploration and mapping.
19. There is no architectural parallel in Colonial New England for the Newport Tower and its specific architectural features.
20. I suggest that the tower was built as a church, observatory, lighthouse, a datum point for future exploration in the New World.

The Order of Construction

Jim Whittall was not the first archaeologist to comment on the odd unit of measurement used in the tower's construction. It has been noted that the diameter of the pillars is 3 feet 1 inch. The width of the wall at the keystone is 3 feet 1 inch. The interior diameter of the tower is 18 feet 6 inches. The distance from the south side of the fireplace to the niche is 1 foot 6.5 inches—odd measurements indeed. Architect Sue Carlson wrote in 1997: "It is inconceivable that English builders, with English tools and rulers would not have used English feet as their unit of measure."[10] The measurement that is peculiar to the Newport Tower that was discovered by Jim Whittall is the Scottish ell. If this is used, the diameter of the pillars measures 1 ell, the interior diameter of the tower is 6 ells, and the exterior diameter is 8 ells. Whittall's research on tool marks proves beyond all doubt that the tower was *not* constructed between 1639, when Newport was founded, and 1677, when it is first mentioned in records. After more than six-and-a-half years of investigation on this site, Whittall concluded that the prime candidate for constructing the Newport Tower is Earl Henry St. Clair.

When we list the most probable dates for the alleged construction of the tower in each of the principal theories and compare that to the list of archival and cartographic references, we can eliminate one major theory. Listing the contenders for the title of builder of the Newport Tower, we have in chronological order of alleged construction:

- The Norse in the tenth century

- Earl Henry St. Clair in the late fourteenth century

- The Corte-Real brothers in the early years of the sixteenth century

- Benedict Arnold shortly after the foundation of the city

We can eliminate the Norse theory, because the Vikings did not use mortar. Following Jim Whittall's research, we too have come to the conclusion that Earl Henry and his men built the tower. Apart from Manuel Luciano da Silva's proposition, there is no credible evidence that the Corte-Real brothers were in this vicinity at all, much less any indication that they could have built the tower. As to the supporters of the Benedict Arnold school, all the archival and mapping references make this concept invalid because all the references predate the colonial era.

Obviously, the majority of those who have studied the tower are in agreement as to its precolonial origin and its distinctively medieval construction. When we run through the conflicting theories as to who built it, the only plausible one that gives a medieval origin is Earl Henry St. Clair. Arlington Mallery's estimate that the tower had been constructed at the end of the fourteenth century confirms Earl Henry St. Clair as the only possible builder. Now, when we take Hjalmar Holand's estimates into consideration, we may be able to make an educated guess as to when it was built. Holand wrote:

> It must have been a colossal task to build the Newport Tower without the aid of beasts of burden, five thousand cubic feet of soil had to be excavated and later refilled. A lime kiln was necessary, and the construction of the building required more than a million pounds of stone, sand and lime, the builders must, therefore, have had plenty of time at their disposal.[11]

From this estimate we can deduce two things: firstly, that the building took place on Earl Henry's second trip across the Atlantic, as we know that he took some Mi'kmaq people with him back to Orkney and returned them in one year, so he would have had sufficient time on mainland America for the construction only during his second visit. Secondly, there must be some archaeological evidence of the construction process left in Touro Park near the tower itself. Furthermore, there may even be some trace of an earlier Viking settlement there when we take into account that Henry was seeking Norumbega. Ground-penetrating radar surveys were made in 1992 and 1994. Bear in mind that before becoming a public park, the area was a hayfield and we have no record of any other building there other than the tower. The results were interesting: over 181 anomalies were found, listed and duly noted, and they vary in depth from 2 to 10 feet. The report of the second survey conducted by the Early Sites Research Society includes the following:

> The Newport Tower does not exist in a void. It has a very definitive relationship with the area that surrounds it; Touro Park. The construction of any structure leaves some evidence of the activity in the immediate area, a dropped artefact, or material waste. Locating the area where the binding mortar was mixed would be of major importance, some dateable organic substance could be retrieved.[12]

All of us, whatever position we have adopted in the dispute over the tower's origins, owe an immense debt of gratitude to the people of Newport, past and present, whose care, pride, and devotion have ensured that this fascinating building has been preserved. Would that all populations adopted a similar attitude to buildings of historical importance instead of allowing them to be demolished in the dubious name of either progress or profit. We can treasure the tower and investigate its origins and meanings, only because Newporters have always done so. We are eternally grateful.

CHAPTER 16

Celebrating History

*This life of man appears for a short space, but of what
went before or what is to follow, we are utterly ignorant.*

—Saint Bede

Antonio Zeno came from an old, aristocratic Venetian family with a
long maritime tradition, and Henry St. Clair was an earl of Viking
descent. Both families had a long relationship with the mystical
order of the Knights Templar throughout its existence. Their voyages to
the New World are indelibly celebrated by permanent mementoes carved
in stone on both sides of the Atlantic that take different forms in a variety of sites. On the American side, the Westford Knight and the Newport
Tower are permanent reminders of their creators, and in Europe, there are
carvings in Rosslyn Chapel near Edinburgh as well as a plaque on the outside wall of one of the Zeno palaces in Venice. Rosslyn Chapel was founded
by the third St. Clair Earl of Orkney—Earl William St. Clair, Henry's grand-
son. Construction began in 1456 and finished at Earl William's death in
1480—twelve years before Columbus crossed the Atlantic in 1492. Now
it is a firm tenet of belief among the official establishment of American
historians that there was no dissemination of American native plants or
animals before the voyage of 1492. How is it, then, that carvings depicting

maize, aloe cactus, sassafras albidium, trillium, grandiflorum, and quercus nigra—all native American plants—decorate this chapel that was completed long before Columbus made his fateful voyage? All of these depictions of new plant life were obviously based on drawings made on Earl Henry's voyage and then brought back to Europe.

The municipality of Venice commemorated the Zeno brothers' voyages in the following words on a plaque mounted on the exterior wall of a Zeno palace:

A

Nicolo e Antonio Zeno

Nel Secolo Decimoquarto

Navigatori: Sapientemente Arditi

Del Mari Nordici

Per Decreto Del Commune

MDCCCLXXXI

[To Nicolo and Antonio Zeno

In the Fourteenth Century

Navigators Fourteenth

of the Nordic Seas

By Decree of the Commune (of Venice)

MDCCCLXXXI (1881)]

These disparate commemorative memorials celebrate all the Zeno/St. Clair voyages, including their exploration of Greenland, their first voyage to America, and their return to Europe. Their second voyage across the Atlantic can be deduced from the oral tradition of the Mi'kmaq that recounts how one of their members was taken to Europe as a guest and returned within one year. The Newport Tower stands as a memorial that this second voyage was prolonged and well prepared to erect the tower. These voyages, important though they were, were *not* voyages of discovery, because they followed the sailing instructions laid down in the Viking sagas. It would be arrogant in the extreme for any medieval or renaissance European to claim to have "discovered" the Americas, especially in light of the many transatlantic and transpacific voyages that we have mentioned in this brief work. The oceans had been crossed and recrossed many times from the end of the Ice Age up to the time of Columbus. Therefore, these questions arise: "Why does Columbus get the dubious credit for discovering America?" and "Why have all the earlier, provable voyages been ignored?" This issue is particularly pertinent when you consider that Christopher Columbus never even set foot on mainland America and also when you answer the question posed by so many Native Americans: "How much land did the white man bring with him when he came?"

Sometimes circumstances combine to mask the emergence of truth in a manner that cannot be blamed on academic bias. Such is the case with the St. Clair/Zeno voyage. There is, for example, an enduring mystery over the details of the death of Earl Henry himself, complicated by the death of Antonio Zeno shortly after his return to Venice in 1405, all exacerbated by the complex story of the compilation and publication of the Zeno Narrative and the resulting controversy about it. All of this has to be taken into account before anyone can pass judgment on the establishment of a U.S. public holiday called Columbus Day.

Let us return to the matter of Earl Henry's death and the ensuing confusion about both the date and the manner of his demise. Earl Henry's life, actions, and movements in both Norway and Orkney are well recorded for most of his life, despite the fact that most of the Orcadian archives were lost at sea at the time of King James III. Henry's death is not mentioned anywhere in either of the state papers of Norway or Scotland, which is a trifle odd to say the least. The few sparse references to it in other sources are confusing and ambiguous. Some years ago my co-author Wallace-Murphy came across this reference to the earl's death in the Advocates Library of the National Library of Scotland:

> [A]nd deit Erile of Orchadie for the defense of the Cuntre was slain their cruelly by his Inimies. . . . of the month of June in the year of our Lord ane hundred 3 and forty sex [date of the document].

> Translated out of Latin into Scots by me Deine Thomas Gwle Munk of Newbothile at the request of ane honourable man William Santclar Barroun of Roslin, Pentland and Herbershire Anno Dom 1554.

Under the signature was the following annotation:

> [T]he true date of this paper appears to be 1406 instead of 1446, the 40 being put with different ink upon the margin, and whereas the spelling here very often varies in the same words, so it is in the original translation from which this is exactly copied.[1]

The wording of the death notice is copied exactly in two other notices with different dates: 1404 and 1400. The 1400 date is recorded by the most unreliable historian of the Sinclairs, Father R. A. Hay, and therefore must be viewed with a considerable degree of caution. The document citing 1404 once resided in the archives of the Earl of Caithness, but the identical nature of its wording and spelling to the one Wallace-Murphy found in the Advocates library is suspicious to say the least. To complicate matters still further, there is yet another document dated 1446 that simply repeats this wording again. Neither the date of Henry's alleged death nor the nationality or nature of his enemies is specified. None of these dates marry up with any raid by the English or the Hanseatic League. The question that arises is "How could the death of such a leading figure fail to be recorded?" Furthermore, there is no record of Earl Henry being buried with his ancestors at St. Matthew's Church at Roslin, nor was his body later reinterred at Rosslyn Chapel, as so many imaginative authors have suggested. There is no record of him being buried either in Orkney or in Norway. Antonio Zeno, who, according to tradition, asked permission to return to Venice several times, eventually arrived there in 1404 and died shortly thereafter. This led Wallace-Murphy to believe that either Henry did not die until 1404 or only then gave Antonio the permission he had sought for so long.

On Henry's death, as was usual, his son (also Henry St. Clair) would have been formally installed as the Earl of Orkney. Although the younger Henry was eventually recognized as the earl, he was never formally installed as such. No one can say why. He was captured by the English and kept in the Tower of London,[2] being released from time to time, with other family members being held as hostage until his return, to allow him to attend to family business in Scotland and Orkney. He left little or no discernible trace on the Islands. He did succeed to the title but was never formally installed. Why? Before Earl Henry's first voyage to America in 1396, Henry drew up a deed that was signed at Roslin by his eldest daughter, Elizabeth, and her husband, Sir John Drummond, wherein they renounced any claim that they might have to any of his lands in Norway as long as Henry had living male heirs.[3] Some scholars have deduced from this that Henry intended to take some of his sons with him on his voyage. If this be so and he had failed to return them, his lands in Norway, including Orkney and Shetland, would pass without dispute to his eldest son, Henry.

The fact that Earl Henry, as senior nobleman in Norway, did not sign the Treaty of Kalmar in 1397 and took no part in the prior negotiations rather indicates that our estimate of the timing of his first transatlantic voyage is correct. He was represented at the negotiations by Bishop Jens of Orkney, who had been appointed in 1396. This was a pivotal treaty that united the three kingdoms of Denmark, Sweden, and Norway under the rule of Queen Margarette, and we suspect the reason that Earl Henry was not present was that, with the queen's blessing, he was engaged on a voyage of exploration that would ultimately extend the reach of her kingdom across the Atlantic. Thus, despite his nonattendance at the negotiations or the treaty signing, he was engaged on matters of supreme importance to his queen. It is impossible to conceive that Earl Henry, who was so meticulous in discharging his obligations to his sovereign and his family, would not have left precise instructions as to the succession to the earldom and to the matter of his own burial. For his death to have been recorded in the strange way we have outlined here is bizarre. Was all this just a matter of camouflage?

We submit that it is highly likely that Earl Henry gave Antonio Zeno permission to go home to Venice and then returned to North America with the firm intention of spending the rest of his life there. As Henry's life amply demonstrates, he was dedicated to the Templar ideals that had pervaded St. Clair family history for centuries—namely, the primacy of communal living, service to others, and the raising of living standards in the community within which he lived. His contacts with the Native American people showed him that here were people who not merely shared similar beliefs but, more importantly, lived them. We would not be at all surprised if that way of life proved infinitely more attractive to the earl than the so-called civilized life in the brutal and intolerant world of late medieval Europe. There is a Native American tradition that tends to confirm this possibility—one that states that the Newport Tower was built by their ancestors as a temple. Thus, if Henry had built the tower and had then been assimilated into the native people of the Narragansett area, this tradition makes total sense. It would also explain two other anomalies recounted by two early explorers. Verrazzano reported on the differing skin colors of the tribes he met between 1524 and 1525. He spoke of one tribe on Rhode Island who had exceptional white skin, and Jacques Cartier mentioned a similar "white tribe" in Nova Scotia. These two areas were visited by the St. Clair/Zeno voyage, one of which may have been settled by Henry himself.

The Deafening Silence after the Voyage

With the death of Antonio Zeno and the "disappearance" of Earl Henry after a "secret" voyage, there was no one left to either promote or publicize it. All that remained in Europe were some drawings of strange plants from the New World and a pile of letters scattered among other documents in the Zeno archive in Venice. They rested there unnoticed and unread for over a hundred years until their accidental rediscovery by a mischievous five-year-old, another Nicolo Zeno, who played with them, scribbled in them, and tore up some of them until stopped by an adult.[4] Later, as a young adult, this Nicolo Zeno reread the portions of those letters he had not completely destroyed and began the slow and tedious task of reassembling these old scraps of aged paper. As he progressed, he began to gain some sort of understanding of the achievements of his ancestors. Fading ink, strange place names, writing in an archaic script, all complicated the issue. Nicolo showed his results to his father, who in his turn showed them to a highly respected relative, Marco Barbaro, who was writing a history of his distinguished ancestors at that time. Barbaro's book, *Discendenze Patrizie*, was published in 1536 and was the first published work to bring Antonio and Nicolo Zeno's exploratory voyages to public notice.

The book was published in several volumes, and in one, we read:

> Nicolo the Chevalier, of the Holy Apostle Parish, called the Old—in 1379 captain of a galley against the Genoese. Wrote with Brother Antonio the voyage to Frislanda where he died.
>
> Antonio wrote with his brother, Nicolo the Chevalier, the voyage to the islands near the Arctic Pole, and of their discoveries of 1390 by order of Zichno, King of Frislanda. He reached the continent of Estotliand in North America. He remained fourteen years in Frislanda, that is four with his brother and ten alone.[5]

Celebrating History

Barbaro's comments had little or no real impact in Europe because his book had only limited circulation within Venice itself. However, within Venice, it was well noted, and several globes from that era show the Zeno landings in Nova Scotia but date them to 1390.

Some twenty years after the publication of Barbaro's work, young Nicolo inherited the letters on the death of his father, and he prepared and published an edited account of his ancestors' voyages and introduced it with the story of how he found the letters as a young child and all but destroyed them. Nicolo's work, now known as "the Zeno Narrative," was published in Venice in 1558 under the rather long title of *The Discovery of the Islands of Frislanda, Eslanda, Egronelanda, Estotilanda and Icaria made by two brothers of the Zeno Family, namely Messire Nicolo, the Chevalier, and Messire Antonio. With a special drawing of the whole region of their discovery in the north.* The special drawing of the whole region of their discovery in the north is a document commonly known as "the Zeno Map." In respect of this map, it is imperative to remember that it was drawn by the publisher of the Zeno Narrative, young Nicolo Zeno, and *not* by either of the original explorers. Like many maps of that period, it contains several parts that were simply copied from other maps and charts—a common practice at that time. The addition of lines of latitude and longitude also caused considerable confusion because they were not calculated in the fourteenth century when the voyages took place. Furthermore, no one in Venice seemed to have any great interest in the Zeno discoveries at the time of the publication of the Narrative in 1558 or even when Antonio had returned in 1404. Why was this?

In John Julius Norwich's superb history of Venice, we learn that by 1405, the time of Antonio's death, Venice had just begun a period of exceptional prosperity and expansion:

> The Republic had become a nation . . . Venice suddenly found herself mistress of a considerable portion of north-east Italy, including the cities of Padua, Vicenza and Verona and continuing westward as far as the shores of Lake Garda. At last, she could treat as an equal with nations like England, France and Austria—in her own right a European power.[6]

With this enormous expansion, the Republic was bent on consolidating and expanding its power and was not about to waste valuable resources and energy on speculative adventures in North America. Mainland Italy was in a state of almost constant war, as a Spanish invading army led by the Duke of Alba threatened the Papal States from one side while an army of over 10,000 Frenchmen led by the Duc de Guise invaded from the other. Venice, commercial as always, sensibly refused to take sides. With the election of Doge Girolamo Priuli in November 1559, Venice's foreign policy problems seemed to evaporate. The Ottoman Turks were in a state of near civil war. However, from the perspective of American exploitation, Venice had missed the boat big time. The pope had divided American spheres of influence between the Spanish and the Portuguese, and Venice could not now crash that particular party. Why then did the Zeno Narrative engender so much controversy?

CHAPTER 17

Controversy over the Zeno Narrative

Then you will know the truth, and the truth will set you free.

—John 8:32

There are two fundamental problems to resolve in evaluating the Zeno Narrative: firstly, the strange names of the places and islands mentioned within it and, secondly, identifying the principal character named in the text, Prince Zichmini. The authors of the letters on which the narrative is based wrote in Italian using information and place names provided by Scots-, Norse-, and Gaelic-speaking people. According to Frederick Pohl, the name Zichmini or Zichmni is "the most troublesome misspelling in history."[1] For nearly two centuries after the publication of the Narrative, no one could even hazard an educated guess at the identity of this mysterious "Prince" until Johann Reinhold Forster identified him as Earl Henry St. Clair in 1784. In a moment of inspired insight, Forster realized that *Zichmini* was a muddled misspelling of *Sinclair*, a popular derivative of *St. Clair*. It was left to Frederick Pohl in the twentieth century to describe the scriptorial mechanism that caused this confusion. His conclusions were confirmed by Professor Barbara A. Crawford, a lecturer in Medieval Studies at St. Andrews University, who confirmed Pohl's interpretation in the following words:

> One has to admit that his [Pohl's] interpretation of "Prince Zichmini" as a misreading of "Principe d'Orkenei" because the Z in Italian script can appear to be d'O is ingenious and on the whole satisfactory.[2]

The principal critic of the Narrative was Fred Lucas, who believed that Zichmini was a Baltic pirate named Wichmann; however, Lucas could not and, more importantly, did not explain how two leading Venetian noblemen, men of the highest repute, would work in conjunction with a pirate and be proud that one of them would be knighted by such a villain.[3]

In 1582, the renowned early historian of the maritime world, Richard Hakluyt, identified six people who reached America before Columbus—and four of these were Venetian. Those four were Marco Polo in 1270, Nicolo and Antonio Zeno in 1380, and Niccolò dei Conti in 1444. In the opinion of historian Jack Beeching, Hakluyt is a most reliable source:

> He was primarily a scholar in the magnificent Renaissance tradition—a man for whom the gratuitous pursuit of knowledge for its own sake was life's most important end. . . . he will go to great lengths to get the facts.[4]

This view was confirmed by another historian, Ben Johnson, who wrote that Hakluyt's writings were "registered for truth."[5]

The state censor of Venice, Ramusio, whose title was "Secretary to the State of Venice," was obliged to ensure the honesty and accuracy of all official publications in the Serene Republic so that nothing could detract from the state's reputation. He interviewed all the ships' captains on their return to Venice and recorded their accounts in detail. He was, therefore, the supreme authority on any voyages, explorations, or travels by any Venetian citizens at that time. As both a historian and a geographer, he was widely known and internationally respected. As noted in Jim Whittall's archive, Professor E. G. R. Taylor of the University of London described Ramusio as "a man who could hardly ever have been deceived." Thus, Ramusio's signature at the bottom of the Zeno Narrative signifies

UNCHARTED

both state approval of the publication and its accuracy insofar as it could be measured. R. H. Major, Secretary of the Royal Geographic Society from 1866 until 1881, described the Zeno Narrative in the following words:

> The first to do himself honour by vindicating the truth of the Zeno Narrative was the distinguished companion of Captain Cook the circumnavigator, Johan Reinhold Forster, in a work published in 1784 and 1786. Amongst others who uphold the narrative we have the following brilliant array of savants: Eggers, Cardinal Zurla, Malte Brun, Walckenaar de la Roquette, the Polish geographer Joachim Lelewel, the Danish Antiquary Bredsdorf also the far-seeing Humboldt.[6]

American historian and author John Fiske wrote a two-volume work, *Pre-Columbian Voyages to America,* in which he wrote:

> In a very true sense Henry [St. Clair], as a civilized man, in the modern sense of civilization, was the one and only discoverer of America; historians of the future are bound to come to this conclusion by all the cannons of criticism. . . . The Zeno Narrative of which there is an English translation in the Hakluyt Societies Collection of Voyages has had full discussion and complete acceptance.[7]

Professor E. G. R. Taylor of the University of London wrote:

> The authenticity of the account [of the Zeno Narrative] has been challenged but on very flimsy grounds. It appears to the present writer to be quite out of the question that any author could invent a story, which in every detail reflects facts about which it is impossible that he could be aware.[8]

Professor William Herbert Hobbs of Michigan University described the Zeno brothers as "reliable and honest explorers who were far in advance

Controversy over the Zeno Narrative

of their age. . . . True they did not reveal a New World to the Old World as Columbus did, but their presence there must be accepted as historical fact."[9] Girolamo Ruscelli described Nicolo Zeno as "an authority in both history and geography . . . universally held to have few equals in the whole of Europe."[10] The world-famous *Encyclopedia Americana* has accepted the Zeno Narrative in editions from 1904 to the present day, and the *Dictionary of National Biography* also confirms that it was Earl Henry St. Clair who led the Zeno expedition. Professor E. G. R. Taylor of the University of London put her finger right on the button when she said that there was no way any Venetian nobleman writing in 1558 could have described the monastery in Greenland, the hot springs nearby, the harbor at Guysborough, and the smoking mountain at Stellarton without firsthand reports from those who had actually been there. Furthermore, there is proof in stone at both sides of the Atlantic: the Westford Knight and the Newport Tower in North America and the carvings at Rosslyn Chapel in Scotland, which stand as mute but incontestable evidence of the truth of the Zeno Narrative, to say nothing of the traditions maintained by the Sinclairs and the Mi'kmaq people whose fraternal amity lasts to this day.

The strangely named islands that seem to have disappeared since the Zeno Map was published are another intriguing puzzle. We need to remember that the map was not drawn by the original explorers but was created when young Nicolo reassembled the letters to form the Narrative. At that time he wrote:

> I thought it good to draw a copy of these northern lands from the sailing chart, which I find I still have among our family heirlooms. To those who take pleasure in such things, it will serve to throw light on what would be hard to understand without it.[11]

Thus, we can see that the rather dubious provenance of this map is based on one that has no connection to the original voyages with which it is associated. It has certainly caused more confusion than clarity. To the chart he used he then added the strangely named lands mentioned in the Narrative proper. When we examine maps or charts of the north Atlantic, most of them cannot be found. Some critics, who have given the Zeno Map and the Narrative the same origins, understandably discount both, thereby throwing the baby out with the bathwater. However, these critics ignore the fact that many of these so-called vanished islands were indeed mentioned by earlier explorers. For example, Estotiland, Estland, and Drogio can be found in Norse and Viking accounts and appear on the Modena Map of 1350.[12] Arlington Mallery made the discovery that clarifies this vexatious issue and authenticates the Zeno Narrative. There had been an island group situated between Iceland and Greenland known as "Gunnbjörn's Skerries." Discovered by the Norwegian trader Gunnbjörn Ulfsson in 920 CE they were described in a book named *Description of Greenland* published in 1873. They are still shown on charts issued by the now-defunct U.S. Hydrographic Office but no longer appear on normal maps because they now lie 60 fathoms deep, or 360 feet below sea level. They sank due to subsidence and last appeared on maps circa 1600. The main island of this group, Gombar Skaare, was at one time 65 miles long and 25 miles wide; according to Arlington Mallery and Charles Hapgood, it was probably even larger at the end of the fourteenth century and was, in all probability, the island of Icaria named in the Narrative. The Norwegian polar expedition under Fridtjof Nansen concluded that the Faroes and Iceland were once connected by a basalt plateau when the shoreline stood 500 meters above the present level. This Faroe-Icelandic ridge extends beyond Iceland to Greenland, and the southern end of Greenland is still sinking.[13] This wide area of subsidence also explains why the size of Iceland on the Zeno Map is seemingly over large. Arlington Mallery detailed the submergence of several provinces of Iceland that sank under the waters after a series of volcanic explosions that ended in 1380, but the subsidence continued for another one hundred years. Mallery wrote:

> Unaware of the consequent sinking of land and the forming of undersea shelves as the surface of the earth shifted under the weight of glacial ice, they [scholars] have not realised that some landmarks on the Viking trail have vanished under ice and water.[14]

Despite its strange provenance, the Zeno Map, and the chart on which it is based, is in fact extremely accurate. Greenland on the Zeno Map is remarkably accurate when compared with modern maps and charts. Hapgood studied over thirty-eight locations in Greenland, Iceland, Scandinavia, Germany, and Scotland and their relationships to one another on the Zeno Map and was surprised at how they relate to those same relationships in modern charts. European points are surprisingly accurate, and Greenland's and Iceland's references only fractionally less so. For all its strange derivation, the Zeno Map was deemed to be authentic by mapmakers such as Mercator, Ortelius, and by the renowned explorer Martin Frobisher. Thus, despite its long and disputed history, the Zeno Narrative has been accepted by a wide-ranging swathe of distinguished academics, including, among others, Hapgood, Hobbs, the Albany Herald of Scotland, American historian John Clarke Ridpath, Sir Iain Moncreiffe of that Ilk, Michael Gelting (the chief archivist of Denmark), Gad Rausing, Arlington Mallery, John Fiske, Ramusio, Ruscelli, and, of course, Frederick Pohl. The reality of the Zeno/St. Clair voyage is no longer in doubt, and time and ongoing research are revealing more details about it as time goes on. But, what about the man who American academia deems to be the discoverer of America and the results of his voyage in 1492?

CHAPTER 18

Columbus: Discoverer of the New World?

And all I ask is a tall ship and a star to steer her by.

—John Masefield

Today, in the early years of the twenty-first century when Columbus is regarded as a hero and the "discoverer of America," for whom a national holiday has been named in the United States, it is perhaps surprising to learn that for the first three centuries after his death, his memory seems to have been almost erased from the historical record. The only mention of this supposedly important man can be found in the records of legal actions he brought against the Spanish crown for recognition of his services to the state. He was deliberately ignored in Spain and hardly mentioned in the United States until the late eighteenth century. At this point it was becoming apparent that the USA had the potential to become a great power and, as a state, began to develop a sense of tangible identity. Even as late as 1804 when the great Alexander von Humboldt was ending his four-year tour of the Americas, he remarked on the lack of statues and memorials to Columbus. When Washington Irving toured Europe in the 1820s, he came across some recently published Columbus papers in Spain, and in 1828, he published an English translation of them. Irving's account spoke of Columbus as a hero, and his rather hagiographic account was reinforced by that of Samuel Eliot Morison, who again portrayed Columbus as a hero and King Ferdinand of Spain as a villain. The bandwagon was en route to glory. Columbus was in effect crowned as "the King of explorers" at the World's Columbian Exposition that was held in Chicago in 1893—better known as the World's Fair. Columbus began to be portrayed as an "all-American hero," a man of supreme virtue who could do no wrong.

The reality of Columbus's arrival in the West Indies is somewhat different, and so are the long-term consequences that his so-called discovery set in motion. A man of immense greed and self-importance who enslaved many of the native people whom he met, Columbus set in motion what historian David Stanford called "purposeful genocide." Samuel Eliot Morison was in agreement when he wrote that "the cruel policy initiated by Columbus and pursued by his successors resulted in complete genocide."[1] A consensus that has emerged over the last few decades describes Columbus in decidedly unheroic terms. One author wrote:

> Columbus sailed into the Caribbean, not the first but the last in a long line of exploratory mariners—perhaps he was the most ignorant as well as the most destructive in his results of all of them. Within a few years the Atlantic was again being crossed and re-crossed by people from the east, but these latecomers were not peaceful traders who brought an enlightened civilization with them. They came to loot and enslave. What they brought with them were guns, bigotry and epidemic disease. The modern European reign of terror had begun.[2]

Estimates vary as to the exact size of the butcher's bill that the Native American people paid for the invasion triggered by Columbus, because the world after 1492 would never be the same for Native Americans. This date marked the beginning of the long road of persecution and genocide of the indigenous peoples of the Americas. Conservative estimates put the indigenous population of the United States prior to European contact as more than 12 million. Within 400 years, that population was reduced by

98 percent to 237,000. The strange thing is that this hero of U.S. mythology never set foot on the mainland of either North or South America. And, as so many historians have mentioned, he certainly did not come to trade peacefully, but to conquer, enslave, and kill. Some hero.

Those who came before him came to trade, to settle, to be assimilated into local populations, whether they had crossed the Atlantic or the Pacific. Where he landed, Earl Henry St. Clair initiated peaceful relations with the Native Americans that have united the Sinclairs and the Mi'kmaq in peaceful harmony to this day.

We have shown how many peoples and individuals reached the Americas long before Columbus. Let us now take a brief overview of the other so-called facts so beloved of academic historians in the USA—that there was no interchange of native American plants or animals before 1492.

Carvings of maize found in a variety of temples in Egypt and some depictions of the same plant on pottery predate Christianity by many centuries. Depictions of pineapples in Pompeii, turkeys carved on the west front of twelfth-century Christian cathedrals such as Bremen, North American furs listed in the manifests of north Atlantic traders exporting from Vinland and Markland to Europe. Carvings of maize, aloe cactus, and fourteen other varieties of plants native to the Americas in Rosslyn Chapel completed prior to 1480. The traces of coca contamination found in ancient Egyptian mummies, to say nothing of the transpacific cultural links between South America, Japan, and China—the list is almost endless.

U.S. academics should remember that we are examining world history and not some private fiefdom that is their sole private property to be dealt with as they wish. They need to remove the blinkers of prejudice and evaluate, strictly but dispassionately, all the evidence for transoceanic voyages and not just the few listed here. Above all, if they are to have a national holiday in the U.S., why not pick one that does not insult the Native Americans so obscenely as Columbus Day—it is akin to asking Jewish people to celebrate Hitler. Celebrate those who came in peace and with good intent. Columbus undoubtedly does deserve to be remembered—and when one understands the devastating effects his invasion set in motion, he will be remembered as a highly flawed human being and not as some superhero. America deserves better than this. We all do.

As Simon Schama once mused: "History ought never to be confused with nostalgia, it's written not to revere the dead, but to inspire living. It's our cultural bloodstream, the secret of who we are. And it tells us to let go of the past, even as we honor it; to lament what ought to be lamented, to celebrate what should be celebrated."[3]

With this in mind, let us all remember that those who came before—from the Egyptians, Romans, Norse, all the way through to Earl Henry St. Clair and the brothers Zeno, and those countless others—did not come to conquer.

Notes

Introduction

1. Thompson, G. (1993) *American Discovery*, p. 175. Seattle: Misty Isles Press.
2. Boland, C. M. (1963) *They All Discovered America*, pp. 56–58. New York: Doubleday.
3. Wells, S. (2002) *The Journey of Man: A Genetic Odyssey*, pp. 138–140. Princeton, NJ: Princeton University Press.

Chapter 1

1. Cited by Boland, C. M. (1963) *They All Discovered America*, pp. xiii-xvi. New York: Doubleday.
2. Thompson, G. (2010) *Ancient Egyptian Maize*, p. 43. *lulu.com*.
3. Cited by Bronowski, J. (2011) *The Ascent of Man*. London: BBC Books.
4. Forbes, R. J. (1964) *Studies in Ancient Technology*, vol. VIII, p. 5. Amsterdam, Netherlands: Brill.
5. Bailey, J. (1993) *Sailing to Paradise*, p. 15. New York: Simon & Schuster.
6. Singer, C., et al. (1965) *A History of Technology*, vol. 1, p. 590. Oxford, England: Clarendon Press.
7. Thompson, *Maize*, p. 2.
8. O'Kelly, M. (1989) *Early Ireland*, p. 152. Cambridge, England: Cambridge University Press.
9. Bailey, *Sailing*, p. 23.
10. Bailey, *Sailing*, pp. 30, 31.
11. Edwards, I. E. S., et al. (1970) *The Cambridge Ancient History*, vol. II, pt. 2, p. 214. Cambridge, England: Cambridge University Press.
12. Thompson, G. (1993) American Discovery, p. 143. Seattle: Misty Isles Press.

13. Scripps Howard News Service, March 27, 1991.

14. Thompson, *Maize*, pp. 89–90.

15. Thompson, *Maize*, p. 146.

16. Fell, B. (1989) *America BC*, p. 17. New York: Simon & Schuster.

17. Thompson, G. (2010) *Secret Voyages to the New World*, pp. 10–11. *lulu.com*.

18. Irwin, C. (1963) *Fair Gods and Stone Faces*, p. 203. New York: St. Martin's Press.

19. Vaillant, G. C. (1931) *A Bearded Mystery*, vol. 31, pp. 243–244. New York: Natural History.

20. Bailey, J. (1973) *The God-Kings and the Titans*, p. 75. London: Hodder & Stoughton Ltd.

21. Thompson, *Secret Voyages*, p. 39.

22. Bailey, *Sailing*, p. 28.

23. Sertima, I. (2003) *They Came before Columbus*, p. 136. New York: Random House.

24. Bailey, *Sailing*, p. 28.

25. Fell, *America BC*, pp. 93, 99.

26. Fell, *America BC*, p. 157.

27. Boland, *They All Discovered*, p. 24.

28. Marx, R. F., and D. Rebikoff (1969) "Atlantis at Last?" *Argosy* vol. 369, no. 6.

29. Marx and Rebikoff, "Atlantis?"

30. Joseph, F. (2021) *Atlantis and Other Lost Worlds: New Evidence of Ancient Secrets*. London: Arcturus.

Chapter 2

1. Thompson, G. (2010) *Ancient Egyptian Maize*, p. 176. *lulu.com*.

2. Thompson, *Maize*, p. 12.

3. Thompson, *Maize*, p. 7.

4. Thompson, *Maize*, p. 41.

5. Thompson, *Maize*, p. 67.

6. Thompson, *Maize*, p. 8.

7. Riley, C. L., et al. (1971) *Man across the Sea*. Austin, TX: University of Texas Press.

8. Thompson, *Maize*, p. 1.

9. Thompson, *Maize*, p. 61.

10. Thompson, *Maize*, p. 62.

11. Thompson, *Maize*, p. 91.

12. Inscriptions among the Ramos collection.

13. Bailey, J. (1993) *Sailing to Paradise*, p. 93. New York: Simon & Schuster.

14. Honore, P. (1963) *In Quest of the White God,* p. 200. London: Hutchinson & Co.

15. Sertima, I. (2003) *They Came before Columbus,* p. 138. New York: Random House.

16. Von Wuthenau, A. (1969) *The Art of Terracotta Pottery in Pre-Columbian Central and South America.* New York: Crown Publishers.

17. Wallace-Murphy, T., and M. Hopkins (2004) *Templars in America*, p. 62. Newburyport, MA: Red Wheel/Weiser.

18. Gibson, F. (1974) *The Seafarers: Pre-Columbian Voyages to America,* p. 45. Pittsburgh: Dorrance.

19. Irwin, C. (1963) *Fair Gods and Stone Faces,* pp. 66–71. New York: St. Martin's Press.

20. Thompson, *Maize,* p. 141.

21. Wallace-Murphy and Hopkins, *Templars,* p. 65.

22. McGlone, W., et al. (1993) *Ancient American Inscriptions,* p. 139. Rowley, MA: Early Sites Research Society.

23. McGlone et al. *Inscriptions,* p. 140.

24. McGlone et al., *Inscriptions,* pp. 154, 155.

25. McGlone et al., *Inscriptions,* pp. 251–268.

26. J. Gwyn Griffiths, Letter to Jim Whittall of the Early Sites Research Society.

27. McGlone et al. *Inscriptions,* p. 268.

28. Davies, N. (1979) *Voyagers to the New World,* p. 142. New York: William Morrow & Company, Inc.

29. Cited by Thompson, G. (2010) *Secret Voyages to the New World,* p. 17. *lulu.com.*

30. Collins, A. (2000) *Gateway to Atlantis,* p. 115. London: Headline.

31. James, P., and N. Thorpe (1994) *Ancient Inventions,* p. 350. London: O'Mara Books.

32. Balabanova, S., F. Parsche, and W. Pirsig (1992) "First Identification of Drugs in Egyptian Mummies," *Naturwissenschaften,* vol. 79, p. 358.

33. Balabanova, "First Identification of Drugs," p. 358; also *Research Verifies the Use of Hashish, Cocaine, and Nicotine in Prehistoric Culture,* London: Sage: Sociology of Drugs.

34. TV program in the *Equinox* series, "Mysteries of the Cocaine Mummies," shown by Channel 4 in England in 1996, repeated in 2000.

Chapter 3

1. Marx, R. F. (1993) *In Quest of the Great White Gods,* p. 37. New York: Random House.

2. De Graauw, A. (2016) *From Amphora to TEU*, p. 11. Grenoble, France: Coastal Engineering & Shiphandling.

3. Strabo (1469) *Geographica*, II. 5.12.

4. Marx, *Quest*, p. 51.

5. Latin translation of *De Mundo* (Venice 1521, 3, 392b).

6. Plato (c. 360 BCE) *Timaeus*.

7. Diodorus of Sicily (c. 60 BCE–30 BCE) *Bibliotheca Historia*, 9:19, 20.

8. Cited in Aelian (c. 175–c. 235) *Varia Historia*, 3:18.

9. Plutarch (c. 80) *Lives*.

10. Strabo, *Geographica*.

11. Strabo, *Geographica*.

12. Jordanes (551), *De origine actibusque Getarum*, ch. 1:4, 7.

13. Marx, *Quest*, p. 51.

14. Carter, G. F. (1953) *Plants across the Pacific: Memoirs of the Society for American Archaeology*, p. 62. Cambridge, England: Cambridge University Press.

15. Thompson, G. (2010) *Secret Voyages to the New World*, p. 39. *lulu.com*.

16. Pliny (77), *Natural History*, XIX, ch. 15.

17. Native American Ethnobotany Database: *naeb.brit.org*.

18. Cited by Gibson, F. (1974) *The Seafarers: Pre-Columbian Voyages to America*, p. 19. Pittsburgh: Dorrance.

19. Thompson, G. (1993) *American Discovery*, p. 175. Seattle: Misty Isles Press.

20. Wallace-Murphy, T., and M. Hopkins (2004) *Templars in America*, pp. 65–70. Newburyport, MA: Red Wheel/Weiser.

21. Haywood, J. (1823) *Natural and Aboriginal History of Tennessee*, Nashville: George Wilson.

22. Marx, *Quest*, p. 30.

23. Irwin, C. (1963) *Fair Gods and Stone Faces*, p. 19. New York: St. Martin's Press.

24. Boland, C. M. (1963) *They All Discovered America*, p. 67. New York: Doubleday.

25. Thompson, *American Discovery*, p. 175.

26. Wallace-Murphy and Hopkins, *Templars in America*, p. 124.

27. Thompson, *American Discovery*, p. 175.

28. Marx, *Quest*, p. 315.

29. *New York Times*, June 25, 1985, p. 3.

Chapter 4

1. Elder, I. H. (1990) *Celt, Druid & Culdee*, pp. 131–134. New York: Artisan Publishers.

2. Gibson, F. (1974) *The Seafarers: Pre-Columbian Voyages to America*, pp. 19–22. Pittsburgh: Dorrance.

3. Boland, C. M. (1963) *They All Discovered America*, p. 130. New York: Doubleday.

4. Thompson, G. (1996) *The Friar's, Map of Ancient America*, p. 27. Bellevue, WA: L. Lee Productions.

5. Bernard Assiniwi, Abenaki historiographer, 1973.

6. Stewart, M. J. A. (2000), *The Forgotten Monarchy of Scotland*, p. 30. Rockport, MA: Element Books.

7. Stewart, *Forgotten Monarchy*, p. 19.

8. Wallace-Murphy, T., and M. Hopkins, (2002) *Rosslyn: Guardian of the Secrets of the Holy Grail*, pp. 77, 78. London: Thorsons.

9. Horn, G. (1652) *De Originibus Americanus*, vol 4. The Hague: Adrian Vlacq.

10. Wallace-Murphy, T., and M. Hopkins, (2004) *Templars in America*, pp. 65–70. Newburyport, MA: Red Wheel/Weiser.

11. Cited by Hakluyt, R. (1589) *The Principal Navigations, Voyages, Traffiques, and Discoveries of the English Nation*. London: George Bishop.

12. Deacon, R. (1967) *Madoc and the Discovery of America*, p. 54. New York: George Braziller.

13. Thompson, *Friar's Map*, pp. 31–32.

14. Wallace-Murphy and Hopkins, *Templars in America*, pp. 72–73.

Chapter 5

1. Haywood, J. (1995) *The Penguin Historical Atlas of the Vikings*, pp. 40–42. London: Penguin. See also Roesdahl, E. (1998) *The Vikings*, pp. 83–93. London: Penguin.

2. Sjovold, T. (1985) *The Viking Ships in Oslo*, p. 6. Oslo: Oldsaksamling University.

3. Sjovold, *Viking Ships*, pp. 69–70.

4. Sjovold, *Viking Ships*, pp. 53–68.

5. Sjovold, *Viking Ships*, pp. 10–36.

6. Sjovold, *Viking Ships*, p. 6.

7. Sjovold, *Viking Ships*, p. 58.

8. Sjovold, *Viking Ships*, p. 56.

9. Sjovold, *Viking Ships*, pp. 53–55.

10. Sjovold, *Viking Ships*, p. 56.

11. Hegedüs, R., Åkesson, S., R. Wehner, and G. Horváth(2007). "Could Vikings Have Navigated under Foggy and Cloudy Conditions by Skylight

Polarization? On the Atmospheric Optical Prerequisites of Polarimetric Viking Navigation under Foggy and Cloudy Skies," *Environmental Science, Physics Proceedings of the Royal Society A: Mathematical, Physical and Engineering Sciences,* vol. 463, no. 2080, pp. 1081–1095.

12. Haywood, *Penguin Historical Atlas,* pp. 106, 107.

13. Roesdahl, *Vikings,* pp. 262–276.

14. Roesdahl, *Vikings,* pp. 52, 78.

15. Haywood, *Penguin Historical Atlas,* pp. 40–42; see also Ingstad, H. (1969) *Westward to Vinland,* p. 32. London: Jonathan Cape Ltd.

16. Pohl, F. (1952) *The Lost Discovery: Uncovering the Track of the Vikings in America,* p. 261. New York: W. W. Norton.

17. Thompson, G. (1996) *The Friar's Map of Ancient America,* pp. 51–52. Bellevue, WA: L. Lee Productions.

18. Holand, H. (1962) *Explorations in America before Columbus,* p. 80. New York: Twayne Publishers.

19. Pohl, *Lost Discovery,* p. 105.

20. Pohl, *Lost Discovery.*

21. Ingstad, *Westward to Vinland,* p. 32.

22. Holand, H. (1940) *Westward from Vinland,* p. 61. New York: Duell, Sloan and Pearce.

23. Roesdahl, *Vikings,* p. 90.

24. Pohl, *Lost Discovery,* pp. 15–16.

25. Prytz, K. (1990) *Westward before Columbus,* p. 10. Toronto: Norumbega Books.

26. Pohl, *Lost Discovery,* p. 18–19.

27. Pohl, *Lost Discovery,* p. 21.

28. Pohl, *Lost Discovery,* p. 26.

29. Holand, *Explorations,* pp. 27–32.

30. Holand, H. (1946) *America 1355–1364,* pp. 8–9. New York: Duell, Sloan and Pearce.

31. Pohl, *Lost Discovery,* pp. 39–40.

32. Pohl, *Lost Discovery,* p. 40.

33. Pohl, *Lost Discovery,* pp. 44–46.

34. *The Flateyjarbók.*

35. Pohl, *Lost Discovery,* pp. 47–49.

36. Holand, *Westward from Vinland,* p. 27.

37. Holand, *Westward from Vinland,* p. 29.

38. Prytz, *Westward before Columbus,* p. 20.

39. Holand, *Explorations,* p. 54.

40. Ingstad, *Westward to Vinland,* p. 44.

41. Ingstad, *Westward to Vinland,* p. 45.

42. Ingstad, *Westward to Vinland,* p. 46.

43. Holand, *America,* pp. 213–215.

44. Ingstad, *Westward to Vinland,* p. 92.

45. Ingstad, *Westward to Vinland,* p. 25.

46. Photius (404 BCE), *Excerpt of Ctesias' Indica.*

47. Stein, C. (2021) "Naturalia medieval: identificação, iconografia e iconologia de objetos naturais no final da idade media," pp. 211–241. New York: The Metropolitan Museum of Art.

48. The Danish Royal household (2012) "The History behind the Anointing Throne," *kongehuset.dk.* Accessed August 4, 2022.

49. Raghavan, M., W. Fitzhugh, and E. Willerslev (2014) 'The Genetic Prehistory of the New World Arctic" *Science.*

50. Chiesa, P. (2021) "Marckalada: The First Mention of America in the Mediterranean Area (c. 1340)," *Terrae Incognitae,* pp. 88–106. Abingdon on Thames: Taylor & Francis.

51. Chiesa, *Marckalada,* pp. 88–106.

52. Chiesa, P. (2016) "Ystorie Biblie omnium sunt cronicarum fundamenta fortissima. La 'Cronica universalis' di Galvano Fiamma," *Bullettino dell'Istituto Storico Italiano per il Medio Evo,* vol. 118, pp. 179–216.

53. Magister Adam of Bremen (1073) *Gesta Hammaburgensis,* Ch. 4, p. 38.

54. Anderson, W. R. (1982) *Viking Explorers and the Columbus Fraud,* p. 47. Chicago: Valhalla Press.

55. Ingstad, *Westward to Vinland,* p. 94.

56. First mentioned in *Recherches sur les Voyages et découvertes des navigateurs Normands,* by Pierre Grignon in 1539.

Chapter 6

1. Sorenson, J. L., and C. L. Johannessen (2001) *Scientific Evidence for Pre-Columbian Transoceanic Voyages to and from the Americas.* Philadelphia: University of Pennsylvania Press.

2. Sorenson and Johannessen, *Scientific Evidence,* p. 1.

3. Sorenson and Johannessen, *Scientific Evidence,* p. 2.

4. Quoted in Sorenson and Johannessen, *Scientific Evidence,* p. 3.

5. Quoted in Sorenson and Johannessen, *Scientific Evidence,* p. 3.

6. Quoted in Sorenson and Johannessen, *Scientific Evidence,* p. 3.

7. Quoted in Sorenson and Johannessen, *Scientific Evidence,* p. 3.

8. Meggers, B. (2010) *Prehistoric America: An Ecological Perspective,* 3rd expanded ed., p. xxv. New Brunswick, NJ: Transaction Publishers.

9. Carter, G. F. (1968) *Man and the Land,* p. 111. New York: Holt, Rinehart & Winston of Canada Ltd.

10. Carter, *Man,* p. 111.

11. Bailey, J. (1973) *The God-Kings and the Titans,* p. 225. London: Hodder & Stoughton Ltd.

12. Von Wuthenau, A. (1970) *Pre-Columbian Terracottas.* London: Methuen.

13. Bailey, *God-Kings and Titans,* p. 227.

14. *American Antiquity* (1953), vol. XVIII, no. 3, 2.

15. Von Wuthenau, *Pre-Columbian Terracottas.*

16. As cited by Thompson, G. (2010) *Secret Voyages to the New World,* p. 62. *lulu.com.*

17. Thompson, *Secret Voyages,* p. 63.

18. Pickersgill, B. (1977) "Taxonomy and the Origin and Evolution of Cultivated Plants in the New World," *Nature,* vol. 268, no. 18, pp. 591–594.

19. Menzies, G. (2012) *1421,* p. 248. London: Transworld Digital.

20. Menzies, *1421,* p. 259.

21. Jett, S. C. (1998) "Dyestuffs and Possible Early Contacts between Southwestern Asia and Nuclear America," in Gilmore, D., and S. McElroy, eds. (1998) *Across before Columbus?,* p. 141. Maine: NEARA.

22. Jett, "Dyestuffs," p. 146.

23. "Two Traditions of Ancient Tibetan Cartography," *The Times,* July 8, 1970.

24. Menzies, *1421,* p. 269.

25. Padron, P. (1906) "Un huaco con Caracteres Chinos," *Sociadad Geográfica de Lima,* vol. 23, pp. 24, 25.

26. Sorenson, J. L., and M. H. Raish (1994) *Pre-Columbian Contact with the Americas across the Oceans: An Annotated Bibliography.* Provo: Utah Research Press.

27. Storey, A., J. M. Ramírez, D. Quiroz, et al. (2007) "Radiocarbon and DNA Evidence for a Pre-Columbian Introduction of Polynesian Chickens to Chile," *Proceedings of the National Academy of Sciences,* vol. 104, no. 25, pp. 10335–10339.

Chapter 7

1. Fossier, R., et al. (1997) *The Cambridge Illustrated History of the Middle Ages, vol. 3, 1250–1520,* p. 65. Cambridge, England: Cambridge University Press.

2. Norwich, J. J. (2003) *A History of Venice*, p. 200. New York: Vintage Books.

3. Norwich, *History*, p. 4.

4. Norwich, *History*, pp. 623, 631.

5. Norwich, *History*, p. 77.

6. Runciman, S. (1951) *A History of the Crusades*, vol. 1, p. 312. Cambridge, England: Cambridge University Press.

7. Norwich, *History*, pp. 79, 80.

8. Albert of Aix (c. 1100) *Historia Hierosolymita VII 225*, pp. 521–523.

9. Bridge, A. (1982) *The Crusades*, p. 205. London: Franklin Watts.

10. Norwich, *History*, pp. 122, 123.

11. Norwich, *History*, p. 128.

12. Bridge, *Crusades*, p. 231.

13. Robinson, J. (1992) *Dungeon, Fire and Sword*, p. 322. London: M. Evans & Company.

14. Robinson, *Dungeon*, p. 323.

15. Norwich, *History*, p. 203.

16. Norwich, *History*, p. 207.

17. Norwich, *History*, p. 197.

18. Norwich, *History*, p. 212.

19. Norwich, *History*, p. 250.

20. Norwich, *History*, p. 253.

Chapter 8

1. Gade, J. A. (1950) *The Hanseatic Control of Norwegian Commerce during the Late Middle Ages*, p. 1. Leiden, Netherlands: E. J. Brill.

2. Larson, L. (2017) *Canute the Great*, p. 288. Chicago: University of Illinois Press.

3. Gade, *Hanseatic Control*, p. 16.

4. Holand, H. (1946) *America 1355–1364*, pp. 8–11. New York: Duell, Sloan and Pearce.

5. Holand, *America*, pp. 11–15.

6. Bredsdorff, J., and C. Pingel (1838) *Grönlands Historiske Mindesmerker*, vol. II, pp. 459–464. Copenhagen: Trykt i det mallingske bogtrykkeri.

7. Pohl, F. (1952) *The Lost Discovery*, p. 196. London: Norton.

8. Translation of the original letter published by the Smithsonian Institution, *Miscellaneous Collections*, vol. 116, no. 3, p. 20.

9. Holand, H. (1962) *Explorations in America before Columbus*, p. 157. New York: Twayne Publishers.

10. Holand, *Explorations*, p. 160.
11. Holand, *Explorations*, p. 166.
12. Nilsestuen, R. M. (1994) *The Kensington Runestone Vindicated*, pp. 7–10. Ann Arbor: University of Michigan Press.
13. Holand, *Explorations*, p. 256.
14. Holand, *Explorations*, p. 278.
15. Holand, *Explorations*, p. 279.
16. Holand, *Explorations*, p. 286.
17. Thompson, G. (1996) *The Friar's Map of Ancient America*, p. 107. Bellevue, WA: L. Lee Productions.

Chapter 9

1. de St. Clair, L. A. (1905) *Histoire Généalogique de la Famille de Saint Clair et des Alliances*, p. 15. Paris: Hardy and Bernard.
2. Dde St. Clair, *Histoire Généalogique*, p. 16.
3. Wallace-Murphy, T., and M. Hopkins (2002) *Rosslyn: Guardian of the Secrets of the Holy Grail*, p. 200. London: Thorsons.
4. Stewart, M. J. A. (2000) *The Forgotten Monarchy of Scotland*, pp. 65, 150. Rockport, MA: Element Books.
5. de St. Clair, *Histoire Généalogique*, p. 18.
6. de St. Clair, *Histoire Généalogique*, p. 19.
7. Scottish Advocates Library, *Genealogical and Topical Manuscripts*. vol. 22, no. 2, p. 9.
8. Pohl, F. (1951) *Prince Henry Sinclair*, p. 10. Halifax: Nimbus Publishing.
9. Sinclair, Lord H. (1590) *The Chartulary of St. Giles, AD 1362: The Descent and Pedigree of the Most Noble and Ancient House of the Lords of Sincleer*.
10. Sinclair, N. (1998) *Beyond any Shadow of Doubt*, Sections 2 & 6. London: Private Publication.
11. Sinclair, *Shadow of Doubt*, section 10.
12. Pohl, *Prince Henry*, p. 27.
13. Sinclair, *The Chartulary of St Giles*.
14. Clouston, J. S. (1932) *A History of Orkney*. Kirkwall, England: W. R. Mackintosh.
15. Pohl, *Prince Henry*, p. 30.
16. Clouston, *A History*, pp. 234–237.
17. Linklater, E. (1965) *Orkney and Shetland: An Historical, Geographical, Social, and Scenic Survey*, p. 73. London: Robert Hale.

18. Hay, Father R. A. (1690) *Genealogie of the Sainteclaires of Rosslyn.*
19. Pohl, *Prince Henry,* p. 43.
20. Pohl, *Prince Henry,* p. 48.
21. Cited by Sinclair, A. (2002) *The Sword and the Grail,* p. 125. Edinburgh: Birlinn Ltd.
22. Torfeus, T. (1711) *Orcades seu Rerum Orcadensium Historia,* p. 177. Copenhagen: Havniae; see also C. Lange (1848) *Diplomatorium Norvegicum,* vol. 55, no. 460, p. 358. Oslo: P. T. Malling.

Chapter 10

1. Linklater, E. (1965) *Orkney and Shetland: An Historical, Geographical, Social, and Scenic Survey,* p. 73. London: Robert Hale.
2. Pohl, F. (1951) *Prince Henry Sinclair,* p. 57. Halifax: Nimbus Publishing.
3. *Icelandic Annals,* 1382.
4. Forster, J. R. (1786) *History of the Voyages and Discoveries Made in the North,* p. 178ff. Oxford: University of Oxford Press.
5. Pohl, *Prince Henry,* pp. 65, 66, 76.
6. Jansen, K. L., J. Drell, and F. Andrews (2009) *Medieval Italy: Texts in Translation,* p. 159. Philadelphia: University of Pennsylvania Press.
7. Pohl, *Prince Henry,* p. 34.
8. Sinclair, N. (1998) *Beyond any Shadow of Doubt,* Section 10. London: Private Publication.
9. Sinclair, *Shadow of Doubt.*
10. Pohl, *Prince Henry,* p. 68.
11. Lange, C. (1848) *Diplomatorium Norvegicum,* vol. 55, no. 515, p. 396. Oslo: P. T. Malling.
12. Pohl, *Prince Henry,* p. 76.
13. Major, R. H. (1873) *The Voyages of the Venetian Brothers, Nicolo and Antonio Zeno, to the Northern Seas in the XIVth Century,* aka The Zeno Narrative, p. 4. New York: Franklin.
14. Pohl, F. (1950) *The Sinclair Expedition to Nova Scotia in 1398,* p. 9. New South Wales, Australia: Picton: Advocate Press.
15. Major, *Voyages of the Venetian Brothers,* p. 6.
16. Pohl, *Prince Henry,* p. 83.
17. Major, *Voyages of the Venetian Brothers,* p. 10.
18. Pohl, *Prince Henry,* p. 85.
19. Cited by Clouston, J. S. (1914) *Records of the Earldom of Orkney.* Edinburgh: Edinburgh University Press.

20. Saint-Clair, R. W. (1898) *The Saint-Clairs of the Isles*, p. 98. Auckland: Brett.

21. Original document is housed in the National Records Office in London.

Chapter 11

1. Pohl, F. (1951) *Prince Henry Sinclair*, p. 91. Halifax: Nimbus Publishing.

2. Sinclair, N. (1998) *Beyond any Shadow of Doubt*, Section 10. London: Private Publication.

3. Major, R. H. (1873) *The Voyages of the Venetian Brothers, Nicolo and Antonio Zeno, to the Northern Seas in the XIVth Century*, aka The Zeno Narrative. New York: Franklin.

4. Pohl, *Prince Henry*, p. 95.

5. Major, *Voyages of the Venetian Brothers*, p. 16.

6. Major, *Voyages of the Venetian Brothers*, p. 20.

7. Pohl, *Prince Henry*, p. 102.

8. Sinclair, *Shadow of Doubt*, Section 10.

9. Major, *Voyages of the Venetian Brothers*, p. 25.

10. Major, *Voyages of the Venetian Brothers*, p. 30.

11. Pohl, *Prince Henry*, p. 113.

12. Major, *Voyages of the Venetian Brothers*, p. 31.

13. Major, *Voyages of the Venetian Brothers*, p. 31.

14. Major, *Voyages of the Venetian Brothers*, pp. 31, 32.

15. Pohl, F. (1950) *The Sinclair Expedition to Nova Scotia in 1398*, pp. 33–34. New South Wales, Australia: Picton Advocate Press.

Chapter 12

1. Davis, S. A. (1997) *Mi'kmaq*, p. 5. Halifax: Nimbus Publishing; see also Paul, D. (2007) *We Were Not the Savages*, p. 5. Halifax: Fernwood Publishing Co. Ltd.

2. Paul, *We Were*, p. 5.

3. Paul, *We Were*, pp. 5, 7.

4. Paul, *We Were*, p. 9.

5. Hoffman, B. G. (1955) *The Historical Ethnography of the Micmac of the Sixteenth and Seventeenth Centuries*. Berkeley: University of California Press.

6. Paul, *We Were*, p. 7.

7. Whitehead, R., and H. McGee (1983) *The Mi'kmaq*, p. 5. Halifax: Nimbus Publishing.

8. Whitehead and McGee, *Mi'kmaq*, p. 8.

9. Brown, L. B. (1997) *Two Spirit People: American Indian Lesbian Women and Gay Men.* New York: Haworth Press.

10. Paul, *We Were,* p. 19.

11. Paul, *We Were,* Chapter 5.

12. Davies, N. (1979) *Voyagers to the New World,* p. 11. New York: William Morrow & Company, Inc.

Chapter 13

1. Major, R. H. (1873) *The Voyages of the Venetian Brothers, Nicolo and Antonio Zeno, to the Northern Seas in the XIVth Century,* aka The Zeno Narrative, p. 33. New York: Franklin.

2. Major, *Voyages of the Venetian Brothers,* p. 32.

3. Major, *Voyages of the Venetian Brothers,* p. 32.

4. Wallace-Murphy, T., and M. Hopkins (2004) *Templars in America,* p. 122. Newburyport, MA: Red Wheel/Weiser.

5. Information given personally to Niven Sinclair by Mi'kmaq representatives at the Sinclair Symposium in Orkney in 1997.

6. Hodgman, Rev. E. R. (1883) *History of the Town of Westford, in the County of Middlesex, Massachusetts,* p. 306. Westford, MA: The Westford Town History Association.

7. Whittall, J. (1980) *T. C. Lethbridge–Frank Glynn, Correspondence 1950–1966,* p. 1. Sutton: Early Sites Research Society.

8. Whittall, *Correspondence,* pp. 31, 32.

9. Wallace-Murphy and Hopkins, *Templars in America,* p. 129.

10. Whittall, *Correspondence,* p. 51.

11. Moncreiffe, Sir I. (1967) *The Highland Clans,* pp. 160–162. London: Bramhall House.

12. Moncreiffe, *Highland Clans,* final paragraph.

13. Their report is in the Jim Whittall archive and was also mentioned in an article in the *New Haven Register* in 1965.

14. Whittall, *Correspondence,* p. 61.

15. Erected by the Clan Gunn Association.

16. Letter from Joseph A. Sinnot to the Archaeological Commissioners of the Commonwealth of Massachusetts to support the preservation of the Westford Knight.

Chapter 14

1. Conant, K. J. (1954) "Yankee Explores the Legend of the Old Newport Tower," *Yankee Magazine*, p. 25.

2. Gibbs, G. (1933) *The Gibbs Family of Rhode Island and Some Related Families*. New York: Private Publication.

3. R. G. Hatfield (1879) article in *Scribner's Magazine*.

4. Conant, "Yankee Explores," p. 25.

5. Reference found in the James Whittall Archive, Newport Tower file, 1940–1960.

6. Reference found in the James Whittall Archive, Newport Tower file, 1940–1960.

7. Photocopied article written by Hjalmar R. Holand in an unnamed magazine dated April 1953, vol. 12, no. 2, p. 62, found in the James Whittall Archive, Newport Tower file, 1940–1960.

8. Conant, "Yankee Explores," p. 25.

9. Conant, "Yankee Explores," p. 25.

10. *Newport History*, vol. 68, pt. 2, 1997, p. 65.

11. Whittall, J., and Carlson, S. (1997) *The Architecture of the Newport Stone Tower*. Chapter 2. Newport, RI: Newport Monograph.

12. Means, P. A. (1942) *Newport Tower*, p. 9. New York: Henry Holt and Company.

13. Means, *Newport Tower*, pp. 9–12.

14. Carlson, S. (1997) *New England Historical Restorations*. Found in the James Whittall Archive, Newport Tower file, 1991–2000.

15. See file "Comparative Studies between the Newport Tower and Round Churches in Europe" contained in the James Whittall archives.

16. Wallace-Murphy, T., Hopkins, M., and G. Simmans (2000) *Rex Deus: The True Mystery of Rennes-Le Chateau and the Dynasty of Jesus*, p. 121. Shaftesbury, England: Element Books.

17. Rafn, C. C. (1842) *Mémoire sur la découvertes de l'Amérique au dixième siècle*. Copenhagen: J. D. Quist.

18. All the comments here can be found in the document *Newport Stone Tower, Comments by European Architects and Historians* in the Jim Whittall archive.

19. *Annual Report of the Board of Regents of the Smithsonian Institution* (1953), p. 391.

20. Thompson, G. (1993) *American Discovery*. Seattle: Misty Isles Press.

21. Siggurson, E. "The Newport Tower," an article published by the *American-Scandinavian Review* found in the James Whittall Archive, Newport Tower file 1971–1980.

22. Notes on the Newport Tower by Magnus Hrolf in the James Whittall Archive, Newport Tower file, 1991–2000.

23. Pohl, F. (1961) *Atlantic Crossings before Columbus,* p. 190. New York: Norton & Co; see also Sinclair, A. (1993) *The Sword and the Grail,* p. 141. Edinburgh: Birlinn Ltd.

24. Notes on the Newport Tower by Magnus Hrolf in the James Whittall Archive, Newport Tower file, 1991–2000.

25. Mallery, A. (1958) "The Pre-Columbian Discovery of America: A Reply to W. S. Godfrey," *American Anthropologist,* vol. 60, p. 149.

26. Frank Glynn writing in 1961, reference found in the James Whittall Archive, Newport Tower file, 1991–2000.

27. Mallery, "Pre-Columbian Discovery," p. 150.

28. Mallery, "Pre-Columbian Discovery."

29. Holand, H. (1946) *America 1355–1364,* p. 36. New York: Duell, Sloan and Pearce.

30. Mallery, "Pre-Columbian Discovery," p. 150; and Holand, H. (1962) *Explorations in America before Columbus,* p. 212. New York: Twayne Publishers.

31. The original copy of the Plowden Petition is in the National Records Office in London.

32. Pohl, F. (1952) *The Lost Discovery,* pp. 182–184. London: Norton.

33. Means, P. A. (1942) *Newport Tower,* p. 9. New York: Henry Holt and Company.

34. Channing, G. G., (1868) *Early Recollections of Newport, Rhode Island: From the Year 1793 to 1811,* p. 270. Newport, RI: Nichols and Noyes.

35. Lossing, B. J. (1855) *The Pictorial Field-Book of the Revolution,* p. 65. New York: Harper & Brothers.

36. Sinclair, N. (1998) *Beyond any Shadow of Doubt,* Section 10. London: Private Publication.

37. Means, *Newport Tower,* pp. 19–21.

38. Channing, *Early Recollection,* p. 270.

39. *The Old Mill at Newport: A New Study of an Old Puzzle,* Jim Whittall archive.

40. Lossing, *Pictorial Field-Book,* p. 66.

41. The preceding passages are paraphrased from an article "Finding for the Portuguese," published in *Medical Opinion and Review,* March 1967.

42. Hawthorne, N. (1837) "Antiquities of North America by John Stark Esquire," *American Magazine of Useful and Entertaining Knowledge,* vol. 3.

Chapter 15

1. Godfrey, W. S. (1951) "Digging a Tower and Laying a Ghost," pp. 5–7. (PhD dissertation, Harvard University).
2. Godfrey, "Digging a Tower," pp. 10–14.
3. Mallery, A. (1958) "Brief Comments," *American Anthropologist,* no. 60, p. 147.
4. Mallery, A., et al. (1956) *The Newport Tower.* Newport: Newport Historical Society.
5. Mallery et al., *Newport Tower,* p. 148.
6. Article by James L. Guthrie, "Comments on the Radio-Carbon Dating of the Newport Tower," in the Jim Whittall archive.
7. Letter to Jim Whittall, dated June 21, 1996, in the Jim Whittall archive.
8. Letter from Professor Andre de Bethune published in *Newport Daily News,* on July 8, 1997.
9. Letter from Professor Andre de Bethune published in the *Newport Daily News,* July 8, 1997.
10. Carlson, S. (1997) *New England Historical Restorations.* Found in the James Whittall Archive, Newport Tower File 1991–2000.
11. Holand, H. (1962) *Explorations in America before Columbus,* p. 240. New York: Twayne Publishers.
12. Wallace-Murphy, T., and M. Hopkins (2004) *Templars in America,* p. 168. Newburyport, MA: Red Wheel/Weiser.

Chapter 16

1. Manuscripts. 32, 2, 41, The Advocates Library, National Library of Scotland.
2. Sinclair, A. (1856) *A Sketch of the History of Roslin and Its Possessors.* Edinburgh: Irwin, Maxwell, Dick.
3. Drummond, W. (1831) *Genealogy of the House of Drummond,* p. 91. Edinburgh: A. Balfour.
4. Pohl, F. (1951) *Prince Henry Sinclair,* p. 177. Halifax: Nimbus Publishing.
5. Barbaro, M. (1536) *Discendenze Patrizie,* final vol. S–Z. Venice: Barbari.
6. Norwich, J. J. (2003) *A History of Venice,* p. 280. New York: Vintage Books.

Chapter 17

1. Pohl, F. (1970) "Prince 'Zichmini' of the Zeno Narrative," *Terrae Incognitae,* vol. 2, no. 1, pp. 75-86.
2. Crawford, B. (1974) *Review of Pohl's Prince Henry Sinclair.* Aberdeen: Centre for Scottish Studies.

3. Lucas, F. (1898) *The Annals of the Voyages of the Brothers Nicolò and Antonio Zeno in the North Atlantic about the End of the Fourteenth Century and the Claim Founded Thereon to a Venetian Discovery of America: A Criticism and an Indictment.* London: H. Stevens, Son & Stiles.

4. Beeching, J., and R. Hakluyt (1982) *Voyages and Discoveries*, p. 19. London: Penguin.

5. Beeching and Hakluyt, *Voyages*, p. 28.

6. Major, R. H. (1873) *The Voyages of the Venetian Brothers, Nicolo and Antonio Zeno, to the Northern Seas in the XIVth Century*, aka The Zeno Narrative, p. vi. New York: Franklin.

7. Fiske, J. (1894) *Pre-Columbian Voyages to America*, p. 237. New York: MacMillan.

8. Taylor, E. G. R. (1964) *A Fourteenth Century Riddle and Its Solution*, pp. 106–107. New York: American Geographical Society.

9. Hobbs, W. H. (1951) "The Fourteenth Century Discovery of America by Antonio Zeno," *Scientific Monthly*, no. 72, pp. 21–31.

10. Ruscelli, G. (1564) *Ptolemy's Geographia*. Venice: Giordano Ziletti.

11. Major, *Voyages of the Venetian Brothers*, p. xxxvi.

12. Thompson, G. (1996) *The Friar's Map of Ancient America*, p. 169. Bellevue, WA: L. Lee Productions.

13. Hapgood, C. (1966) *Maps of the Ancient Sea Kings*, p. 152. New York: E. P. Dutton.

14. As cited in A. Mallery, and M. Roberts (1951) *The Rediscovery of Lost America*, pp. 138–140, 163–166. New York: E. P. Dutton.

Chapter 18

1. As cited in Stannard, D. (1992) *American Holocaust*, p. xii. New York: Oxford University Press.

2. Bailey, J. (1993) *Sailing to Paradise*, p. 61. New York: Simon & Schuster.

3. *Simon Schama: A History of Britain*, BBC Documentary, 2010, Episode 15, Closing Remarks.

Index

A

Adam of Bremen, 56
Alaric the Goth, 70
Albany Herald of Scotland, 172
Aldred, C., 15
Allen, F. J., 134
Allison, G., 61
alluvial tin, 4, 7
Álvares Cabral, P., 33
America BC (Fell), 39
Amerindian rock art, 21
amphorae findings, 32–33
Andersen, M., 45
archaeology, ground rules for, 1–2
Aristotle, 29
Ari the Learned, 46
Arnold, B., 136–137, 153
Arsenale, 72, 74
Assiniwi, B., 37
Attila the Hun, 70

B

Baardson, I., 56–57, 83, 85, 106
Bailey, J., 63
Balabanova, S., 24
Barbarigo, G., 78
Barbaro, M., 107, 163–164
Bar Kokhba Revolt (132-135 CE), 31
Beauchop, E. R., 125

Beeching, J., 168
Biggart, N., 128
Bimini Road, 8–9
Black Death, 76
Black Hoof (Shawnee chief), 40
boatstone, 127–129
Boehringer, H., 31
Book of Lismore, The, 36
Book of the Dead, The (papyrus scroll), 16
Borden Cook, H., 139
Bradley, B., 2
Brazilian Historical and Artistic
  Institute of Rio de Janeiro, 33
Brønsted, J., 134
Bronze Age, 3, 4
bronze development, 4

C

Cambridge (UK) Antiquarian Society,
  124
Cambridge University Museum of
  Archaeology and Anthropology, 124
Caradoc of Llancarfan, 39, 41
carbon dating, 33, 63, 147–149
Carlson, S., 133, 152
Carmichael, M., 24
Carter, H., 16
Cartier, J., 162
Casson, L., 29

Celer, M., 29
Celtic Christianity, 38
Celts, 35–41
  Christianity and, 38
  Paradise discovery, 36, 37
    saintSt. Brendan the Navigator,
      35–38
    trans-atlantic exploration authors,
      38–39
    transatlantic travel of, 36–37
    Welsh traditions, 39–41
Channing, G. C., 137
Charles the Bald, 38
Chiesa, P., 53, 55
Chioggia, 77–78
Christmas, P., 22–23
Chronicle of Spaine (Siculus), 30–31
Clan Sinclair Association, 112
Clarke, C., 122
Clouston, J. S., 89, 91
Cnoyen, J., 85
Columbus, C.
  American flora/fauna transmission
    by, 11–12
  Atlantic voyage of, 1–2
  depictions of, 173–174
  Egyptian contact with Americas
    pre 1492 voyage of, 11–25 (*see
    also* corn in Egypt; Egyptians in
    Americas)
  historical record of, 173
  Native Americans and, 174–175
  questions concerning America
    discovery, 159
  remembering, 175–176
Conant, K. J., 132
Connecticut Archaeological Society,
  124
Constantinople, sack of, 73–75
copper

  artifacts in North American burial
    mounds, 5–6
  New World deposits of, 3–4
  transatlantic trade of, 5–7
  use of, in Americas, 4
corn in Egypt, 11–18
  ancient Egyptian farming of, 15
  carvings of, in Egypt, 175
  isolationist/diffusionist meaning
    of, 11
  Old World maize, 13–15
  Punt voyages and, 16–18
  Thompson discoveries of, 15–16
cornrow farming, 15
Council of Ten, 75
Cram-Sinclair, N., 95
Crawford, B. A., 167–168
Cronica Universalis, of a *"terra que
  dicitur Marckalada"* (Galvaneus), 53
Cuevas, M., 23

D

Darling, S., 61
da Silva, M. L., 138, 153
David, R., 24–25
David II, King of Scotland, 88–89
Davies, N., 118
de Arde, A., 89, 91, 95–96
de Bethune, A., 148–149
de Bouillon, G., 71, 72
de Candolle, A., 11, 12
de Carvalho, E., 33
de Cavalli, G., 78
de Gray, W., 71
dei Conti, N., 168
de Mézières, P., 89
Department of Classical Greek History,
  University of Massachusetts, 32
Description of Greenland, 171
Dictionary of National Biography, 170
diffusionist beliefs, 11–12, 13

UNCHARTED

"Digging a Tower and Laying a Ghost" (Godfrey dissertation), 145–146

Discendenze Patrizie (Barbaro), 107, 163–164

Doria, P., 77

Drummond, J., 161

E

Earl Henry. *see* saintSt. Clair, H., Earl of Orkney

Early Sites Research Society, 32, 149, 154

Easton, G., 146

Egyptians in Americas, 13–25
    bearded face carvings and, 19–20
    drug discoveries and, 24–25
    hieroglyphics discoveries of, 22–23
    oceangoing vessel carvings of, 16–17
    Olmec civilization and, 17–19
    petroglyphs on USA cave walls and, 20–22
    photographs/artifacts depicting, 15–16
    plant species discoveries, 13–16
    tobacco discoveries and, 23–25

Einarsson, G., 57

Ekholm, G., 64

Elizabeth I, Queen, 40

Encyclopedia Americana, 170

equinoctial sites, 20

Eratosthenes of Cyrene, 29

Eriksson, L., 48–49, 51, 54

Eriksson, T., 49–50

Erik the Red, 48, 54

Erlendsson, H., 47

F

Færeyinga Saga (Viking saga), 46

false beard symbol, 20

Farley, G., 20

Fell, B., 39

Ferguson, T. S., 22

Fiske, J., 169, 172

Flateyjarbók (Viking saga), 46, 47, 50, 85

Fleming, W., 41

Forbes, R. J., 3

Forster, J. R., 167

Frobisher, M., 172

Frolen, H., 134

Fuller, T., 38

G

Gagne, A. J., 125

Galvaneus (Galvano) de la Fiamma, 53–56

García Payón, J., 31

Gardner, J., 40

Gelting, M., 172

German merchants, 81–82

Gibbs, W., 146

Gibson, F., 19

Gillespie, R., 20

Gladwin, H. S., 6

Glooscap, 119

Glynn, F., 124–125, 128

Gnupsson, E., 56–57

Godfrey, W. S., 145–146

Gonzalez, M., 23

Goodwin, W. B., 38–39, 124

Great Lakes of North America, 4

Greenland, maritime trade and, 82–83

Griffiths, J. G., 21

Gumilev, L., 66

Gunn, J., 127, 128

Gunnbjörn's Skerries, 171

Guthrie, J., 21

Guthrie, J. L., 147–148

H

Haakon IV, King of Norway, 81
Haakonson, Haakon (King of Norway), 57
Haakon VI, King of Norway, 92
Hakluyt, R., 41, 168
Halyburton, J., 89
Hanseatic League (Hansa), 69–70, 82, 92
Hapgood, C., 171, 172
Hatfield, R. G., 132
Hauksbók (Viking saga), 46, 47
Hay, R. A., 160
Haywood, J., 31
Heinemeir, J., 147–148
Hendrickson, C., 135
Herjulfsson, B., 48
Heyerdahl, T., 12, 37
Hildreth, A., 127
Historia Cambria, 39
Historia de la Nacion Mexicana (Cuevas), 23
History of Technology, A (Singer), 3
History on the Rocks (TV documentary), 20
Hobbs, W. H., 106, 111, 169–170, 172
Hodgman, E. R., 124
Holand, H., 47, 48, 49, 83–85, 132, 153–154
Homer, 7
Honoré, P., 63
Horsford, E. N., 12, 132
Howe, J., 32
Howieson, J., 146
hunter-gatherer societies, 2

I

Il Leone (the Lion), 78
Ingstad, H., 56
IPHAN, 33
Irving, W., 173–174

Íslendingabók (Viking saga), 46–47
Isle Royale, 4
isolationist beliefs, 11–12, 13

J

Jelic, L., 106
Jerusalem, fall of, 72–73
Johannessen, C. L., 59–60, 61
Johnson, B., 168
John W. Higgins Armory, 125
Jonsson, H., 99
Joseph, F., 8
Junger, H., 147–148

K

Karlsefni, T., 47, 50–51
Kelley, D., 21
Kensington Runestone, 84–85
Knights Hospitaller, 74
Knights Templar, 74, 79–80, 157
Knutson, P., 83
Koch, L., 106
Kuznetsov, B., 66

L

Lake Superior, 4
Larsen, H., 106
Lascot, M., 23–24
La Serenissima, foundation of, 70–73
Leonard, P., 20, 21
Lethbridge, T. C., 124, 125–126
Libby, W. F., 149
Lines, M., 128
Linklater, E., 95
Lixus site, 8–9
longship, 44–45
Lossing, B. J., 136, 138
Lucas, F., 168

M

Madoc ab Owain Gwynedd, Prince, 39–41
Maillard, P., 23
maize, 13–15. *see also* corn in Egypt
Major, R. H., 169
Mallery, A., 40, 136, 146–147, 153, 171, 172
Mandan people of North Dakota, 40
Margarette, Queen of Norway, 57
Maritime provinces, 113
maritime trade in Europe. *see* Mediterranean maritime trade; Western coasts maritime trade
Marx, R., 8, 32–33
McGlone, W., 20, 21
McKay, L. F., 111
Mediterranean maritime trade, 69–78
  Black Death and, 76
  Chioggia and, 77–78
  Constantinople, sack of, 73–75
  continuous war and, 76–77
  La Serenissima, foundation of, 70–73
  overview of, 69–70
  Venetian trading network, 75–76
Meggers, B., 12, 62–63
Mena, D. R., 66–67
Menzies, G., 12
Mercator, 172
Merrill, E. D., 30
metallurgy, developments in history of, 3–4
Mi'kmaq people, 113–120
  communication means of, 117–118
  districts of, 113–114
  flag controversy, 118–119
  lands of, 115–116
  sex among, 116–117
Minoans, 6
  travels of, 6–7

Monahan, S., 20
Moncreiffe, I., 126–127, 172
Monte Alban temple site, 19–20
Morison, S. E., 12, 174

N

Nansen, F., 171
Naval Oceanographic Institute, 33
Navigato Sancti Brendani (the Voyage of St. Brendan), 36
Nero, 30
Newport Tower, 131. *see also* Old Stone Mill at Newport, Rhode Island
New World
  early visitors to, 1
  resources, trade commerce and, 3–4
New World Foundation, 22
New World Isolationist Paradigm, 12
Nicholas of Lynne, 85
North Atlantic exploration, 105–112
Norway, maritime trade and, 80–81
Norwich, J. J., 74, 76, 164

O

ocean crossing, 5–8
Oceanographic Institute of Rio Grande, 33
Odoric of Pordenone, 56
Olaf II, King of Norway, 56
Old Stone Mill at Newport, Rhode Island, 131–143
  age, origin, and use controversy of, 131–135
  architectural design of, 133–134
  builder theories of, 136–139
  de Bethune on, 148–149
  Godfrey on, 145–146
  Guthrie on, 147–148
  Mallery on, 146–147
  order of construction in, 152–155

pre-colonial references to, 135–136

Skeleton in Armor discovery and, 139–143

Watchman on, 148

Whittall findings, 149–152

Olmec stone heads, 18–20

Omara, H. J., 127

Originibus Americanus, 39

Orkneyinga Saga (Viking saga), 46

Ortelius, 172

P

Paradise discovery, 36, 37

Paul, D., 120

Pausanias, 29

Pearson, M., 124–125, 128

Pederson, A., 106

Phoenicians, 6

travels of, 6–8

Phoenician tablet, 7

Pickersgill, B., 65

Pisani (Admiral), 77, 78

Plato, 29, 30

Pliny, 30

Plowden, E., 136

Plutarch, 29

Pohl, F., 48, 96, 105, 106, 109–110, 119, 122, 127, 167, 172

Polansky, J., 20

Polo, M., 56, 168

Polunin, N., 62

Pre-Columbian Voyages to America (Fiske), 169

Prince Henry Sinclair Association of North America, 112

Punt voyages, 16–18

R

Rafn, C., 134

Ramses II, Pharaoh, 23

Ramusio, censor of Venice, 168–169, 172

Rausing, G., 172

Rebikoff, D., 8

Richardson, E. A., 132

Ridpath, J. C., 172

Rifaud, J. J., 14

Rita Joe, Dame, 119–120

Ritchie, J., 119

Robert the Bruce (King of the Scots), 69, 88

Roman Empire, ancient Greeks and, 27–33

amphorae findings, 32–33

boatbuilding skills of, 27

cargo vessels of, 28

cross-Atlantic travel by, 27–28

early writings of islands west of Atlantic, 29–30

evidence of, in Americas, 30–32

ship size, compared to Santa Maria, 28–29

shipwrecks off coast of Americas, 32

silphium disappearance and, 30

Rosslyn Chapel, 157

Ruins of Great Ireland in New England, The (Goodwin), 38–39, 124

Ruscelli, G., 170, 172

S

Sahure, Pharaoh, 17

Severin, T., 37

sheela-na-gig, 20

Siculus, M., 29, 30–31

Sigurðsson, H., 134–135, 138

silphium disappearance, 30

Sinclair, H., 89

Sinclair, N., 105, 128

Sinnot, J. A., 128–129

Skeleton in Armor discovery near Newport Tower, 139–143

Smith, J., 135–136

Snefru, Pharaoh, 14
Solutrean hypothesis, 2
Sorenson, J. L., 59–60, 61
Spera, M., 91, 95–96, 98
Stanford, D., 2, 174
Stark, J., 140–142
saintSt. Brendan the Navigator, 35–38
    Paradise discovery, 36, 37
saintSt. Clair, H., Earl of Orkney, 22, 57,
    87–94
    agreement with Jonsson, Bailiff of
        Norway, 98–99
    as Baron, 88–90
    coat of arms, 97–98
    controlling moves made by,
        103–104
    death of, 159–162
    family connections of, 95–96
    Glooscap relationship with, 119
    history of, 87–88
    installation document, 91–92
    Newport Tower and, 153, 154
    pledge to the Crown, 93
    sea power of, 96–102
    secret voyage of, 163–165
    Vinland voyage, 121–129
saintSt. Clair, T., 95
saintSt. Clair, W., baron of Roslin,
    87–88
Stirling, M., 18–19
Stolp, C., 23
stor-houses, 127–128
Strabo, 29
Strongbow, 35
Studies in Ancient Technology (Forbes), 3
Svarvasson, G., 47

T

Tarshish ships, 7
Tartessian, 7–8
Taylor, E. G. R., 168, 169

Teixeria, R., 32
Templars in America, 120
Terrae Incognitae (Chiesa), 53
Theopompus of Chios, 29
"Westford Knight," 123–127
Thompson, G., 5, 15–16, 19, 23, 86, 134
Thorbrandsson, S., 50
tin, 4, 7
transatlantic trade, 6–7
transpacific contact, 59–67
    A. duodenale presence and, 61–62
    China links to Americas, 63–66
    evidence of, 59–60
    Meggers Japanese ceramics find
        and, 62–63
    Valdivian pottery an, 63
    Tryggvason, O., 48
two-spirit people, 116
two-way river, 6

U

Ulfsson, G., 171
Unicorn Herald, 126
unicorns, 51–52
Ursus of Heraclea, 71

V

Van Sertima, I., 12
Venetian trading network, 75–76
Venice, Mediterranean trade and. see
    Mediterranean maritime trade
Verrazzano, 135, 162
Verrill, R., 6
Victorian era, 2
Vikings, 43–57
    culture, 45–46
    described, 43
    Eriksson voyage, 49–50
    Galvaneus and, 53–56
    Iceland discovery, 47–48
    Karlsefni exploration, 50–51

longship and, 44–45
North Atlantic exploration by, 47–49
sagas, 46–47
shipbuilding techniques, 44–45
unicorn chasing by, 51–52
Vinland church records and, 56–57
Vinland church records, 56–57
Vinland voyage
boatstone and, 127–129
saintSt. Clair, H., 121–123
Westford Knight and, 123–127
Vita Brendani (the Life of Brendan), 36
von Heine-Geldern, R., 31, 64
von Humboldt, A., 173
von Wuthenau, A., 19, 64

W

Wadsworth Atheneum of Hartford, Connecticut, 124
Wallace-Murphy, T., 39, 63, 105, 111, 112, 118–119, 128, 149, 160
Watchman, A., 148
Welsh traditions, 39–41
Wendish group, 69–70
Western coasts maritime trade, 79–86
German merchants and, 81–82
Greenland and, 82–83
Hanseatic League and, 82
Kensington Runestone translation, 84–85
Knights Templar and, 79–80
Norway and, 80–81
We Were Not the Savages (Paul), 120
Whittall, J., 21, 127, 128
Whittall, J. P., Jr., 149–152, 153, 168
Wilde, O., 1
Will, E., 32
Wilson, I., 47
Wood, W., 136

Z

Zeno, A., 108, 157, 168
death of, 159, 161
Zeno, C., 77, 78, 89, 100–101, 108
Zeno, N., 22, 101–102, 164, 168
North Atlantic exploration, 105–112, 158
Zeno Map, 170–172
Zeno Map, 170–172
Zeno Narrative, 101–102, 164
controversy over, 167–172
hot springs described in, 106
landfall identification, 111–112
Mi'kmaq people and, 113–120
smoking mountain investigation, 109–111
Zheng H., 12
Zimmer, H., 38
Zolo, L., 120

About the Authors

Tim Wallace-Murphy (1930–2019) studied medicine at University College, Dublin, and then qualified as a psychologist; he then became an author, lecturer, and historian. He wrote or cowrote more than a dozen books, including *Templars in America*, *The Mark of the Beast* (with Trevor Ravenscroft), *Rex Deus*, and *Rosslyn: Guardian of the Secrets of the Holy Grail*. This last book provided invaluable source material to Dan Brown for his best-selling novel, *The Da Vinci Code*. Tim was a dedicated supporter of the restoration and preservation of Rosslyn Chapel, near Edinburgh, Scotland, undertaking excavations and field work with a team of like-minded people, who would become lifelong friends.

James Martin is a British trade unionist, historian, economist, and lecturer, having previously worked in finance and employment law, and now is a lecturer in further and higher education. As a historian, James believes that "understanding the past is crucial to understanding our future," noting that evidence should guide us, but our minds should be open to ideas. James has studied a wide range of fields, including industrial relations, equalities, history and politics, occupational safety and health, and astronomy, and has recently completed a DEd to further his role as a lecturer. James has taught for a number of academic institutions, ranging from Ruskin, Oxford, to Northern College.

James has been a member and investigator of the Worsley Paranormal Group since its founding in 2003. He has made numerous appearances on radio and television and is now a regular on NightVision Radio. He has described himself as a history geek and a space nerd and has dedicated a large portion of his more recent life to research into the Knights Templar, the Roman Empire, and the Western traditions of spirituality. The motto that guides his research is G.O.Y.A. (Get Off Your Ass), which is why you are more likely to find him out in the field.

www.newrennies.org